Divine Warrior Training

Manifesting the Divine in our World

Thomas F. Capshew, Ph.D.

Innerspark Press

Bloomington, Indiana

Copyright © 2009 by Thomas F. Capshew

Published and distributed by:
Innerspark Press
P.O. Box 2244
Bloomington, Indiana 47402-2244 USA

www.innersparkpress.com

Cover and jacket design: Theresa Venezia

All rights reserved. No part of this book may be reproduced by any process, including mechanical, auditory, photographic or electronic, nor may it be stored in a retrieval system, transmitted or otherwise copied for public or private use without prior written permission of the publisher. Brief quotations may be utilized in articles and reviews under the "fair use" doctrine.

This book does not dispense medical, psychological, or spiritual advice or prescribe the use of any technique for treatment of physical, emotional, mental, or spiritual problems, either directly or indirectly. Readers are encouraged to consult with a licensed professional for your specific issues. The intent of the publication of this book is to provide general information for spiritual well-being. You have the constitutional right to use the information in this book as you wish, and the author and publisher assume no responsibility for your actions.

Library of Congress Cataloging-in-Publication Data

Capshew, Thomas
 Divine warrior training: manifesting the divine in our world / Thomas F. Capshew. - - 1st ed.
        (cataloging information pending)

ISBN 978-0-9801346-3-6 (paperback)

11 10 09 08   4 3 2 1
1st edition, November 2008

Printed in the United States of America

Divine Warrior Training

To the divine essence within each of us

Contents

Acknowledgements xv

Introduction xvii

Section I:

Chapter 1:   The Divine Game: A New Cosmology 1

Chapter 2:   Understanding Evil, Fear and Love 23

Chapter 3:   Divine Warriors 37

Chapter 4:   Healing Ourselves 59

Chapter 5:   Healing Others 81

Chapter 6:   Healing the World 93

Chapter 7:   A Few Words for the Christians among Us 105

Section II:

42 Exercises to Assist in Discarding Limiting Beliefs and Patterns

Expanded Contents

Acknowledgements xv

Introduction xvii

Section I:

CHAPTER 1:   The Divine Game: A New Cosmology 1
         ***Essence:** "We are all divine."*
         Order:
         a. The divine as a pool of water
         b. The divine as an organism
         c. The divine game
         d. The evolution of human consciousness
         e. The fall
         f. Transcending dualistic worldviews

CHAPTER 2:   Understanding Evil, Fear and Love 23
         ***Essence:** "We are all good and we are all evil."*
         Order:
         a. Illusion of separateness
         b. How we come to evil ways
         c. Fear is the soil from which evil grows
         d. Divinity is the soil from which love grows
         e. Our legacy – the inner spark within the
              sacred heart

CHAPTER 3: Divine Warriors 37
   Essence: "We are all preprogrammed with purpose, skills and challenges."
   Order:
   a. Axis mundi
   b. Closing the gap
   c. Living in the trinity
   d. Trinity of relationships
   e. Relationship with self
   f. Relationship with other
   g. Relationship with divine

CHAPTER 4: Healing Ourselves 59
   Essence: "We are all wounded."
   Order:
   a. Finding our spiritual essence
   b. Being human means being wounded
   c. Transforming our wounds
   d. Self forgiveness
   e. Exhaling our limitations, inhaling our potentials
   f. Comfort as holding our healing breath

CHAPTER 5: Healing Others 81
   Essence: "We can all create conditions for healing."
   Order:
   a. Letting go of judgment
   b. Stigma is collective fear
   c. Minimum conditions for human existence
   d. The greatest gift
   e. Compassion in our daily lives

CHAPTER 6:   Healing the World 93
    Essence: "We are all the problem and we are all the solution."
    Order
    a. Divine warriors as stewards
    b. Becoming a steward
    c. Living as steward
    d. Ascent to the mountain top

CHAPTER 7:   A Few Words for the Christians among Us 105
    Essence: "Just as the divine cannot be contained, we have multiple paths to relationship with the divine."
    Order
    a. Relationship with self
    b. Relationship with other
    c. Relationship with divine
    d. The messiah agenda
    e. Living out our common legacy with Jesus

Section II:

EXERCISE 1:	Your Personal Cosmology
EXERCISE 2:	Viewing Your Life from the Moon
EXERCISE 3:	My Life Review
EXERCISE 4:	Contact with the Other Side
EXERCISE 5:	"To Die For"
EXERCISE 6:	Self Forgiveness
EXERCISE 7:	Parts of the Whole
EXERCISE 8:	Job
EXCERCISE 9:	Both Masculine and Feminine
EXERCISE 10A:	Holistic Model - Physical (Part 1 of 4)
EXERCISE 10B:	Holistic Model - Intellectual (Part 2 of 4)
EXERCISE 10C:	Holistic Model - Emotional (Part 3 of 4)
EXERCISE 10D:	Holistic Model - Spiritual (Part 4 of 4)
EXERCISE 11:	Mirrors
EXERCISE 12:	What Feeds You and What Drains You
EXERCISE 13:	A Burger and a Salad
EXERCISE 14:	Exile
EXERCISE 15:	Polarities
EXERCISE 16:	On Your Heels or On Your Toes
EXERCISE 17:	The Problem of Evil
EXERCISE 18:	Evil in the Spiritual World
EXERCISE 19A:	Defining Evil (Part 1 of 4)
EXERCISE 19B:	Defining Evil (Part 2 of 4)

Exercise 19c:	Defining Evil (Part 3 of 4)
Exercise 19d:	Defining Evil (Part 4 of 4)
Exercise 20:	Absolute Evil
Exercise 21:	Evidence of, and Beliefs about, Evil
Exercise 22:	Making Sense of Spontaneous Remission
Exercise 23:	The Empty Chair
Exercise 24:	What is a Miracle?
Exercise 25:	Breath as Healing
Exercise 26:	The Blessing is Next to the Wound
Exercise 27:	Illness as a Metaphor
Exercise 28:	Laughter is the Best Medicine
Exercise 29:	Speaking Authentically #1
Exercise 30:	Speaking Authentically #2
Exercise 31:	Your Persona versus Your True Self
Exercise 32:	Speaking Truth
Exercise 33:	Giving It All Up
Exercise 34:	The Divine Moves in Mysterious Ways
Exercise 35:	Be Still
Exercise 36:	Who Cares?!
Exercise 37:	Assessing Your Connection to the Divine
Exercise 38:	Finding the Weak Link
Exercise 39:	Rules for Discernment
Exercise 40:	Choosing a Path of Love
Exercise 41:	The Divine 2 x 4
Exercise 42:	Tuning in to the Messages all around You

Acknowledgements

ALL OF MY LIFE EXPERIENCES have brought me to the point of writing this book and the perspective it contains. Accordingly, I am grateful to every soul who has crossed my path in my life, both for the joys and challenges. If I were to focus my gratitude on specific individuals, it would be first, on my wife and wonderful support, Pamela. Next, on two souls who chose me to be their father in this journey, Julia and Maclaine. Finally, on Greg, who consistently insisted I needed to write down the way I see and live my life.

INTRODUCTION

ABOUT ME

THANK YOU FOR PICKING UP THIS BOOK. I am grateful you are taking the time to read these words. Please let me tell you a little about myself so you can get an idea of where I am coming from, especially as it relates to spirituality. I was raised in a fundamentalist Christian family. Both my parents were religious, and I attended and grew into their church. At a young age, I "accepted Jesus Christ as my Lord and Savior," attending church faithfully and doing my best to follow the church's teachings.

After high school, I attended a college affiliated with the church, and settled on double majoring in Bible and Biblical Languages. All of my life has been focused on understanding why we exist and finding meaning in this experience we call life. The summer between my Junior and Senior year in college, I had a crisis of faith. The question I kept asking everyone who would listen was this: Assume there is a man in the jungles of Brazil who has lived his life with love and generosity, similar to the qualities Jesus encouraged. Further, assume this man never heard of the name Jesus, nor knew anything about Christianity. When this man dies, where would he spend eternity? Every single person in the church to whom I posed this question said the same thing: this man would burn in Hell because he had not accepted Jesus as his Savior. My crisis in faith came because I could no longer reconcile the teachings of the church with my concept of a loving God. I could find no fairness, no justice, and no love in the answers I received from the church. From that moment, I discarded all Christianity, indeed all religion, and lived my life with little or no compass to guide me.

However, I found the drive to the divine within me

unrelenting. Over time, I began to see truth and value in spiritual paths, purposely shying away from organized religions. Indigenous traditions caught my interest with their reverence for the earth and their respect for others. Their rituals felt somehow familiar. Buddhism came next, with the freedom of finding my own way through a private meditation practice instead of signing on to a particular dharma or tradition. Hinduism followed closely behind, especially with the concept of maya, life being the great illusion. Hinduism seems to have a certain freedom of practice with so many representations of the divine from which to choose. Each faith tradition I examined held the essence of the same truth – the true path is the path of love.

My everyday life took on the same lack of compass that characterized my spiritual life. I finished college, owned a small business, went to law school and practiced law successfully for seven years. Realizing that law did not make my heart sing, I went back to school and earned a Masters in Social Work and a doctorate, hoping that teaching social work would make my heart sing. After a few years of teaching, it began to dawn on me that I was not yet home – I had not yet found my calling.

Divine Warrior Training

A few years ago, I began writing down things that were not my own thoughts. The best way to describe the experience is that the things I was writing down came *through* me. I would wake up around 4:00 in the morning with several pages to type. One day, a friend invited me to a sculpture studio and set me up with a blow torch and a large sheet of metal. As I stood there trying to think of what to attempt to create, the symbol you see on the cover of this book was burned into the metal in front of me by my own hand as though directed by some unseen force.

Many people have asked me what the symbol means. I respond by turning the question back to them: what do you see in it? Take a few moments, if you will, to look into it for your own vision.

For me, the symbol has shown itself as many things, sometimes morphing from one to the next: a mask, a tree, a bird, a human, a cross, a narrow passageway. It continues to reveal itself to me.

Over time, the words and the symbol coming through me have come into focus as this book. The book you are holding in your hand is what I have come to know is the reason I was born – to

Introduction

bring to full term and then to birth these words, put together in this way for this time.

Writing this book has been a deeply personal experience. In writing this book, I looked deep inside myself and inside my views to find the truth of my experience. When I was centered in my divine essence, the words came easily and I knew whether they came from my heart or my head. If they came from my heart, they were my truth. If they came from my head, they were from the ego that I have constructed to navigate the world. To the best of my ability, this book comes from my heart and is offered to you with the humility born from walking my path and deep respect for your path. I have come to understand, through the process of writing this book, that whether anyone else finds the material useful, it was certainly useful to my life to get clear about my values and how I strive to live them.

While writing is deeply personal, publishing a book is equally intimate. It is a process of allowing oneself to be vulnerable. The more I put myself into the book, the more exposed I became to anyone who chooses to read it. While I cannot control the intent with which you read this book, I can request that you read it with an openness to my intent in writing it. That intent, stated succinctly, is to bring more light, life and love into the world, particularly among and between humans. If this book accomplishes that purpose for you, I am delighted. If it does not, please lay it aside or pass it on, and I wish for you a short search for the book or experience that will open you up to all the possibilities that life has to offer.

For me, I feel I won the lottery when I was born. I was born male, White, Middle Class, Christian and American; no physical impairments, a generally loving and supportive family with two parents. Each of these identities is highly valued in the dominant society. None of these I consciously chose and most I could not revoke even if I wanted to. Each identity comes with great privilege, and that is how most of the world sees it. Life for someone with all these identities should be "a piece of cake." But it is not, at least it has not been for me. I had opportunities to settle, to live out the values around me. But something inside of me continued to be restless - I needed meaning and purpose, not just comfort. Comfort did not bring peace for me. The framework set forth in this book has brought that peace.

I bring to this book a unique collection of events that has

occurred over my lifetime. I also bring to this collection of events a unique perception of those events, including their meaning and interrelatedness. Events that occur in our lives, seen through the lens of our perception, equal the experiences that shape us. We often have choices of both events and perceptions, thereby completing the feedback loop of our lives: experiences shape us and we shape experiences. At bottom, I believe we have a choice to see life as suffering and pain or as beauty and joy. My unique experiences (events and perceptions) have given me ample opportunity to head in either direction, toward suffering and pain or toward beauty and joy. I have chosen the latter, finding that my life works better for me when I look for the beauty and joy of life rather than feeling taken over by suffering and pain. This, for me, is the essence of the path of a Divine Warrior: looking for beauty and joy in the world and using all opportunities to expand my life into greater light, life and love.

About the Book

WE LIVE IN THE BEST OF TIMES. Never before has humankind had so much power and potential at its collective disposal, giving us the possibility of creating peace and prosperity for all. We live in the worst of times. Never before has humankind had so much power and potential at its collective disposal, giving us the possibility of perpetuating violence and trauma of unparalleled magnitude. Each of us makes meaning of our experiences through our world view, or cosmology. A cosmology has embedded within it values that drive the choices we make. Our cosmology is the choice point for using humankind's power and potential to benefit all or to wreak havoc.

Religious traditions provide cosmological frameworks. Sciences and philosophies, as well as ethnic life ways and nationalities, can offer cosmologies. As the longstanding boundaries between people in our world erode and evaporate, the cosmologies which helped us to make sense of human experience have lost their utility. In fact, many of our cosmologies are now causing more harm than good: Christianity versus Islam, Israel versus Palestine, and numerous conflicts involving one ethnicity, religion, or sect against another.

Our old cosmologies are dragging us down into conflict instead of raising us up into our potential. Now is the time for a new way of viewing the world that transcends the insignificant ways we are different from one another and reminds us of our common heritage, no matter where the accident of our birth places us. This book is humbly offered as a start toward a new cosmology that simultaneously transcends all the conflicts over the ways we might be different and distills the essence of all our faith traditions. This book offers a path toward light, life and love: a path that I call Divine Warrior Training.

DIVINE

HOW DOES ONE LABEL SOMETHING that is no "thing" and is at the same time everything? Humans have struggled with this question since we first began to communicate, sometimes even going to war over the names used. Some of the names in use today include:

God	Source
Allah	Force
Universe	Yahweh
Creator	Great Mother
Spirit	Chi
Tao	

For many of us, some of these names trigger emotional reactions, pleasant ones and unpleasant ones. Pleasant reactions can draw us out and up into a more expansive view of ourselves and the world around us. Unpleasant reactions can bottle us up into a limited and limiting view of ourselves and the world around us. Every name ever used falls hopelessly short of the reality of that which is unnamable. Whatever collection of writings you might regard as holy, the force described therein is infinitely bigger than the words used to describe or name it. Names are a way of providing boundaries around that which is named. How does one put boundaries on that which is, by definition, without boundaries?

There is no way out of this purely human conundrum, especially in a book that invites the reader into a more expansive view of that which is unnamable. To solve this conundrum, at least for purposes of this book, I will use a word for the unnamable that is recognized across most faith traditions and has not been appropriated or closely associated with any faith tradition to the exclusion of others: divine. Please know when I use the word divine, I am referring to everything you or I can imagine, multiplied exponentially to the highest power. All analogies fall short. A grain of sand on the beach imagining all the other grains of sand on that beach or on all beaches in the world is imagining something

Introduction

infinitely smaller than the divine.

For me, the "big" questions of why are we here and the meaning of life have always been at the forefront of my life. One of the first memories I have was feeling joy at being in a body and wondering if tomorrow "I" would be in my brother's body instead of mine. Over the years, I have come to understand the importance of being connected to something greater than ourselves and come to understand that each of us has that drive toward connection, what I call in this book "the drive to the divine." This drive is vastly greater than the differences in the way we label or characterize the divine.

Warrior

WARRIOR TRADITIONS ARE A CONSISTENT APSECT of human history. Our current understanding of the term warrior is equated with going to battle against other humans, mostly men, to protect against perceived threats to our security, however that has been defined and manipulated. Warriors come from both genders. Current use of the term warrior equates a warrior with a soldier, but in the classical sense, their training and consciousness are very different. A soldier is trained to follow the command of her superior officer. A warrior is trained to follow the command of her superior values. A soldier is trained to battle other people who are identified as enemies. A warrior is trained to battle the enemy existing within himself. A soldier is trained to believe that violence may be the best means to advance the cause. A warrior recognizes that violence is always the worst choice to advance the cause. In the end, we are all warriors in the battle for our souls. Many of us are losing the battle because we have lost sight of the only reason we are struggling in the first place: to manifest the divine in this material existence.

My experience has taught me that whatever challenges I face in the world "outside" myself are much less significant and much easier to face than the challenges and fears I find within my own psyche. All of the challenges I have faced in life are related to overcoming my own sense of inadequacy or arise out of my own sense of fear. As I move into a place of connection and peace, the sense of inadequacy and feelings of fear lose their power and control and it becomes easier to choose light, life and love.

Training

GREAT ACCOMPLISHMENTS ARE NOT EFFORTLESS. All of the greatest human accomplishments have taken extraordinary

Introduction

focus and extraordinary energy. Becoming good at anything takes practice and discipline. Becoming a divine warrior is no different - practice and discipline are required. Training does not require perfection or a complete understanding of the ultimate goal; training does require choosing a focus for your energy and then consistent investment of energy over time toward that focus. Consistency and discipline over time are rewarded with a life that becomes abundant and magical.

Where do you invest your energy? Is it focused or unfocused? This book is designed to give us tools to focus our energy on manifesting the divine in this world. It is a book of Divine Warrior Training.

I look forward to meeting you on the path!

Chapter 1

The Divine Game: A New Cosmology

WE ARE THE DIVINE. Not just one of us, as someone with "delusions of grandeur" might believe. Not just some of us, as a fascist or racist or nationalist might believe. Not just those among us who we might consider "enlightened," as some might believe. Not just certain nations, or certain parts of the world, or followers of certain religions as these collections of individuals might believe. Every one of us, and all of us, collectively, together with all that is created, are the divine.

Divine Warrior Training

The divine is you, and me, and the starving child in India, and the father dying of AIDS in Africa, and the CEO of a Fortune 500 company, and Jesus, and an "Islamic terrorist," and our elected officials, and an unborn fetus, and a man scheduled to be executed. As far as the eye can see, and farther, all is the divine. We originate out of, live within, and return to the divine.

The Divine as a Pool of Water

IMAGINE STANDING WAIST DEEP IN A POOL OF WATER. Take your hand and make a splash. If you focus on just one drop of water that has left the pool of water, that is your life. Before you were splashed (born), you were part of the pool of water. For the time you are in the air, you perceive yourself as separate, something different and apart from not only the pool of water, but every other drop of water that has existed before, exists simultaneously with you, or will exist in the future. After the drop of water that we are calling "you" falls back into the pool (dies), you return to the source from which you came. Before the splash, during the trajectory of the drop, and after returning to the pool, your essence is always water. The drop is always source in its essential form.

As humans, we have become fixated on "our own drop of

Chapter 1

water" to the exclusion of almost everything else. We compare "our drop" to "his drop" or "her drop." We mourn when a drop does not successfully leave the water, and we mourn when a drop falls back into the water "too soon." Many of us spend our lives trying to rediscover our connection to the water, and some of us even claim that we are drops of water and other drops of water do not belong to the water unless they agree to our rules. The pool of water has no rules and needs none. Human life is just a brief splash. If a human lives to be 100 years old, most of us consider that span to be a long life. The fact is, when a 100-year-long life is placed in the perspective of time, that 100-year-long life lasts a fraction of the time that a drop of water spends out of the pool.

The divine is a pool of water and each of us is a particle of water, seemingly separated from the divine by evaporation or a splash, spending a brief amount of time in that state of imagined separation, and always returning to our source. Our return to source is as inevitable and natural as a drop of water rising up out of the pool from a splash and falling back into the pool. Our return to source is as inevitable and natural as water particles evaporating from a source, only to collect together in a cloud and fall down as rain to then find their way back to source. Our illusion of separateness, which generates our forgetfulness, keeps us from seeing our place in the divine. We are never separate from the divine; we are never something apart from the divine. We are fashioned out of the stuff of the divine and never become anything less, except in our minds.

The Divine as an Organism

IMAGINE THAT YOU ARE NOT AN INDIVIDUAL HUMAN, but a part of a larger organism. What would be the primary function of your existence? Might you be a part of the organism that moves other substances around, like an over-the-road trucker? Might

> *No man is an island,*
> *entire of itself;*
> *every man is a piece of*
> *the continent,*
> *a part of the main.*
>
> *- John Donne*

you be a part of the organism that responds to trauma and goes to help heal, like a disaster worker or healer? Might you be a part of the organism that generates fuel for the body, like a farmer? Might you be a part of the organism that breaks down fuel into consumable pieces, like a meat processor or food producer? Might you be a part of the organism that helps move the body's waste so that it does

Chapter 1

not accumulate, like a janitor or garbage collector? Or might you be a part of the organism that holds the memory of events that have occurred, like an historian or museum curator? Whatever you do in this world can be analogized to a function of an organism.

Quantum physics informs us that our material world, including humans, is a single undifferentiated energy field, a cosmic soup. We use our visual senses to differentiate a chair from a cat, and this differentiation is nothing more than distinguishing between two vibrational levels of a larger energy field. We are energetically in relationship with everything around us. We are energetically connected to each other in a similar way that the parts of a living organism work together to maintain the health and life of an organism. Extending this analogy, the organism we call humanity is ill and in need of care and healing.

Just as your body is mostly comprised of cells that are helpful for the growth and continued life of the organism, there are some cells that are not beneficial and do not promote growth and health. Sometimes when our bodies are out of balance, these cells can accumulate and begin to compromise the health of the entire organism. The organism's health is dependent upon recognizing these unhealthy cells and minimizing their impact on the organism as a whole. When whole groups of cells grow strong and begin attacking other parts of the body, we call that cancer. War is a cancer in the body of humanity. When someone willfully limits the supply of food to his stomach, we call that anorexia. Not providing the basic survival needs to other humans wherever they are in the world is anorexia in the body of humanity. Heart disease is a leading cause of illness among individuals in our world. We have lost heart in the body of humanity. Whatever we struggle with collectively, it manifests in our individual bodies. Our collective ills as a human species have their corollary to illnesses we experience as individuals. Just as we have become ill collectively, we will only heal collectively.

The Divine Game

THE TOTALITY OF OUR EXISTENCE is the divine playing a game with itself. Since we are all the divine, we are playing a game with ourselves: "the divine game." In the beginning, before time and matter existed, something existed. This something that existed before time and matter we can call consciousness. This consciousness was all pervasive, encompassing everything, without

Chapter 1

boundary. Nothing existed outside of this consciousness. At some point, this consciousness chose to play a game with itself, a game of forgetfulness. Consciousness chose to create matter in a point of singularity, out of which arises all energies and all material things which have existed, exist, and will exist. Just as nothing existed outside of the consciousness existing before matter, no energy or matter which has been created exists outside of this consciousness. In this book, we are labeling this consciousness "the divine."

> *For in him we live, and move, and have our being.*
>
> *- Acts 17:28 (KJV)*

All human history is a record of human attempts to comprehend the divine and reawaken to the divine. All the breakthroughs in philosophy, medicine, technology and every other aspect of human achievement is a movement toward the divine. All of the wars, violence and trauma humans have experienced and visited upon each other are also movements toward the divine. All religions are human attempts to provide a framework for the divine, and all religions, by their very nature, fall short of developing an all-encompassing framework. To borrow a Buddhist phrase, religion is a finger pointing to the moon. The divine is the moon.

Recent research in consciousness studies makes clear that what we perceive as reality is shaped by what we expect to perceive. Our beliefs about the nature of the world shape what we see in the world, creating a self-reinforcing feedback loop. Therefore, what we see in the world is a direct reflection of our current collective cosmology. Our current collective cosmology shows itself in war, poverty, violence, and a general desacralization of each other and our world. Our current cosmology has us in a vicious cycle. We are in dire need of a new, more expansive, more positive cosmology that can inspire us to higher consciousness. We are in need of a cosmology in which we can develop a virtuous cycle.

What might a world look like if we were to start from knowing that we all are the divine? What if we were to start from knowing that our perceived separation from the divine is nothing more than an illusion?

The Evolution of Human Consciousness

THE POOL OF WATER ANALOGY helps in understanding our individual life's relationship to the divine. Many of us spend the bulk of our lives focused on our individual lives, as if we were

Chapter 1

viewing our individuality through a microscope. Let us step away from the microscope for a few moments to see a more expansive view of the path of collective humanity. Keeping in mind that we are in the midst of the divine game - all-encompassing consciousness returning to an awareness of itself - here is one possible view of the process we are living.

The Fall

WE ARE OPERATING OUT OF AN ILLUSION of separateness and incompleteness. Maintaining this illusion are cultural stories that emphasize our "sin" or "fall from grace." As the story goes, after God created humankind, humans lived for a time in a paradise on earth. Both man and woman in their own way disobeyed God and were cast out of the garden, to live broken and mean lives. In the Abrahamic traditions (Jewish, Christian and Muslim), we have shortened the title of this myth to "the fall." From this myth the concept of "original sin" was developed, emphasizing human weakness and separation from God. The essence of Christianity is based on the belief that humans are sinful and need to be saved by God in human form. Beliefs are a combination of thought and emotion.

Divine Warrior Training

Thoughts and emotions are energy. Whatever we invest energy into grows and becomes real. When humans are believed to be sinful and violent, we create sinful and violent humans. Is it surprising that we manifest human violence and hate when we spend so much energy focusing on our sinful nature? Our current cosmology is based on sinfulness, separation and suffering. What is needed is a new cosmology of capacity and connection. The following story is offered in place of the one which no longer serves us:

> *During humankind's early evolution, man and woman lived in unitive consciousness with the divine and all creation. Men and women saw everything as connected and whole. At some point in time, human consciousness developed the ability to separate the world into subject and object, thereby transforming all that is into duality, including the duality of good and evil. As "subject," for the first time humans felt separate and apart from "objects," including the unitive consciousness we call the divine. As humans developed more capacity to view the creation in duality, they felt more and more distant from the unitive consciousness and the other aspects of the created world.*

Chapter 1

Seen in this way, humans become separate from the divine not because of some shortcoming, but due to the development of a new capacity, the ability to differentiate their experiences and see the world through a dualistic lens. Perhaps this event, memorialized in Abrahamic traditions in a negative light, can be viewed as one step in the evolution of human consciousness, an event marking the shift in the divine game from one phase to the next. The following is an overview of the evolution of human consciousness, with examples taken from western faith traditions. Similar examples can be drawn from faith traditions in other parts of the world.

Phase 1: Unitive Consciousness

THIS PHASE OF THE DIVINE GAME begins with the big bang (the point of gravitational singularity) and ends with the development of the capacity of duality in human consciousness. During this phase, humans see themselves as part of everything that is, moving through creation and everything that is without awareness of separateness. The divine is in everything, and everything is divine. Living is not "good" and dying is not "bad," they simply exist, as part of the flow of life. This world is generally represented by what historians have termed maternalistic faith traditions, marked by connection to the earth, natural processes, and connectedness.

Phase 2: Distant Divine

THE SHIFT TO PHASE 2 occurs when human consciousness develops to the point of the capacity for duality. As the capacity for perceiving the world through a duality lens develops and spreads among humans, we collectively forget the unitive consciousness and move into a duality consciousness, perceiving the divine as "object" and "other."

This phase is marked by the faith traditions which view the divine as distant in time and place, powerful and terrible. This transcendent divine is beyond human comprehension and is often seen as arbitrary and capricious. Whether viewed from a one God (monotheistic) model or a many gods (polytheistic) model, the events of the world are explained by attributing human characteristics to the divine. The divine gets angry. The divine chooses certain people over others. The divine demands sacrifice, sometimes even human sacrifice. In this phase the divine was seen as a powerful and terrible force in the world, was perceived as "other," and we believed that the best we could do was to appease this vengeful "other." The faith traditions of this phase are mainly paternalistic, with the more powerful deities having a masculine gender attributed to them.

Phase 3: Divine Among Us

THE ARRIVAL OF JESUS OF NAZARETH is our clearest marker for the shift from the Distant Divine Phase to the Divine Among Us Phase. The teachings of Jesus were a clear departure from a consciousness of the divine as angry, distant and separate.

Central to the teachings of Jesus is that each of us contains the essence of the divine within us. Jesus lived and spoke from a place of humanity's intimate relationship with the divine, from the divine beyond our comprehension to the divine within us. With the benefit of the hindsight of two millennia, we can now see that these teachings were too large of a shift for humankind to collectively make in one step (See Chapter 7 for a discussion of how the essence of Jesus' message was diverted into a framework for men to exercise power over other humans). In Phase 3, we come into a consciousness that recognizes that the divine can be in human form and can live among us. Humans are still sinful and wounded, but there is hope because the divine has shown us a path back to a relationship with the divine. We have seen the divine and he looks like us.

Phase 4: Divine in Us

WE ARE CURRENTLY IN THE MIDST OF A SHIFT from Phase 3 to Phase 4. For the last century or so, there has been a shift to an emerging awareness that our consciousness is unlimited and inextricably connected with all that we perceive. Physics has taught us that nothing can be observed without being impacted by the observer: subject and object are inextricably joined and our perception of separation is an illusion. While philosophy declares that "God" is dead (at least the one outside ourselves), scientific investigation has begun to focus on mystical and unitive experiences: experiences available to all humans.

The final stage of the evolution of human consciousness is recognizing that each of us, individually and collectively, is the divine. We arise out of, live within, and return to the divine. This awakening brings us full circle. But we have created human structures that invite, encourage and support the forgetting of our divine essence. All faith traditions teach the same core tenant: we have divine essence within us, and our task is to remember to live out of that knowing. Currently, discourses about faith are dominated by claims of exclusivity: faith traditions claiming a monopoly on

Chapter 1

truth and the path to the divine. These claims of exclusivity ignore each individual's inherent value emanating from her or his divine essence.

We are moving into Phase 4 as humans shift away from an allegiance to a particular religion toward an interest in spirituality. In Phase 4, we are able to pick and choose the teachings and rituals from various faith traditions by following our own inner wisdom rather than adopting a collection of rules predetermined by external authorities.

The primary purpose of every human born on this planet is to manifest the divine in this material plane. None of us is expendable. None of us is useless for this purpose. None of us has any less purpose. Each and every one of us, no matter what condition, color or culture we are born into, is here for this primary purpose. Each and every one of us is invited in our lives to stray from that primary purpose. The state of our current world is testimony that many of us accept the invitation to stray. And the beauty of being human is that we can choose at any moment to return to our primary purpose, to awaken to what life is truly about, to embrace the divine in ourselves, in others and in all creation.

We are all part of an intricately interwoven dance of divine consciousness. If, in dreams, every part of the dream represents a part of us, then in waking life, every part of our waking lives represents a part of one's self. The homeless man I meet on the street is a representation of a part of me, the person I fall in love with is a representation of a part of me, the person I view as an enemy is a representation of a part of me. And I fulfill the same role for others. We each live at the choice point of reality - we choose to bring more love into the world or more fear into the world - and there is no moment in our lives where we can be neutral with this choice point.

The evolution of human consciousness has parallels in the developmental stages of a single life. In infancy, there is no differentiation between self and other - infants experience their world as an undifferentiated whole. As the child grows, it experiences decisions by its parents as confusing and arbitrary, a somewhat distant power beyond the ability to comprehend. This is consistent with the second stage of the evolution of human consciousness, with the divine beyond the understanding and reach of humans. The scientific revolution can be viewed as the

Chapter 1

adolescence of the evolution of human consciousness, where all authority is questioned, even to the point of questioning the need for the divine at all. We are now at the cusp of transitioning into the adulthood of the evolution of human consciousness, where we recognize that not only is the divine making more and more sense, but we are the divine, the very thing we previously feared and rebelled against.

Transcending Dualistic Worldviews

THIS BOOK IS ABOUT taking our lives out from under the microscope. This book invites us to shift our focus from a single strand of thread to see that the single strand of thread is woven into a beautiful, flowing tapestry. Viewing life as spirit reduced to flesh allows one to move beyond duality - to transcend duality - to come to a knowing that life is not good *or* bad, it is good *and* bad; not beautiful *or* ugly, but beautiful *and* ugly; not awful *or* wonderful, but awful *and* wonderful. Within each and every experience in the material plane lies the seed of the opposite in the pair of duality. We recognize this through some of our truisms: "What does not kill you makes you stronger." "Turn lemons into lemonade." "Turn stumbling blocks into stepping stones."

It is not that dichotomies are useless or negative. Dichotomies serve a useful purpose in helping us navigate the world. We could not leave the room we are in without a long period of trial and error if we are unable to differentiate between the wall and the door (or window). We would not be able to maintain our health without the ability to differentiate between substances our body needs (such as food and water) and substances our body would reject (such as motor oil or poisons). Being able to differentiate and dichotomize is not the problem among humans. The problem is placing a judgment on one or the other end of the spectrum. For example, many people find light to be good and darkness to be bad. Once darkness is seen as bad, the next step is to begin fearing darkness and creating all sorts of monsters to inhabit the space

> *Out beyond ideas of wrongdoing and rightdoing, there is a field.*
> *I'll meet you there.*
>
> *When the soul lies down in that grass, the world is too full to talk about. Ideas, language, even the phrase each other doesn't make any sense.*
>
> *- Rumi,*
> *translated by Colman Barks,*
> *The Essential Rumi, page 36*

Chapter 1

so feared. Darkness, in fact, has much utility. It allows growing organisms to rest (except for nocturnal animals) and allows the atmosphere to cool. Absent the intermittent light and darkness of our world, one side of the planet would be scorching hot and the other would be freezing cold. Darkness then is essential for life and for balancing our world.

> *A successful search for Truth means complete deliverance from the dual throng of love and hate, happiness and misery.*
>
> *- Mohandas K. Gandhi*

In addition, dichotomies allow humans to know the qualities of an experience. One cannot know what beauty is unless one knows what the absence of beauty is. One cannot know joy without knowing sorrow. One cannot know kindness without knowing cruelty. Within the essence of every quality is a seed of the opposite quality.

David Bohm, in his book "Wholeness and the Implicate Order," goes even further with the concept of enfoldment: human minds have created the cognitive ability to view the material world as made up of smaller and smaller parts. Enfoldment, as a theory in physics, suggests that each and every "part" of the material world contains the entire universe within it. In Bohm's view, each of us is a hologram of the entire universe. Not only are we the divine in our essence, but we are the divine in our potential.

Additional Resources for Chapter 1:

1. Barks, Coleman (1995). *The Essential Rumi*. San Francisco: HarperCollins. ISBN # 0-965-064871, www.harpercollins.com

> A beautiful translation of the writings of a Sufi mystic who was in direct relationship with the divine.

2. Bohm, David (1980). *Wholeness and the Implicate Order*. London: Routledge. ISBN # 0-415-11966-9, www.routledge.com

> Although this book is somewhat difficult to digest for a non-physicist, it presents a beautiful vision of how reality can be viewed more expansively as well as humanity's limited ability to see the whole of reality. It is certainly worth wading through!

3. Cousins, Norman (1974). *The Celebration of Life: A Dialogue on Hope, Spirit, and the Immortality of the Soul*. New York: Bantam Books. ISBN # 0-553-35455-8, www.randomhouse.com

> This book is one of the most mind-expanding and optimistic books I have ever read. I cannot recommend it enough!

Chapter 1

4. Eisler, Riane (1987). *The Chalice and the Blade: Our History, our Future*. San Francisco: Harper. ISBN # 0-062-50289-1,

    www.harpercollins.com

    This book presents a history of civilization prior to the currently-dominant male-centered paradigm.

5. Jung, Carl Gustav (1981). *Archetypes and the Collective Unconscious*. New York: Princeton University Press. ISBN # 0-691-01833-2, pup.princeton.edu

    A quotation from this work says it much better than I can:

    > My thesis, then, is as follows: In addition to our immediate consciousness, which is of a thoroughly personal nature and which we believe to be the only empirical psyche (even if we tack on the personal unconscious as an appendix), there exists a second psychic system of a collective, universal, and impersonal nature which is identical in all individuals. This collective unconscious does not develop individually but is inherited. It consists of pre-existent forms, the archetypes, which can only become conscious secondarily and which give definite form to certain psychic contents. p. 43

6. Laughlin, Charles D. Jr., McManus, John, and d'Aquili, Eugene G. (1990). *Brain, Symbol & Experience: Toward a Neurophenomenology of Human Consciousness*. Boston: New Science Library. ISBN # 0-87773-522-0 www.shambhala.com

    This book provides a systematic approach to how our brains create consciousness from the perspective of the discipline of anthropology. (Out of print, but worth locating a copy.)

7. Teilhard de Chardin, Pierre (1965). *The Divine Milieu: An Essay on the Interior Life*. New York: Harper. ISBN # 0-060-93725-4, www.harpercollins.com

> The author comes as close as a Catholic priest can come to declaring the universe as God and Christ without being excommunicated. He has several other excellent books.

Chapter 2

Understanding Evil, Fear and Love

WE ARE ALL INHERENTLY GOOD. We choose life, light and love if we perceive unrestricted choice. This choosing of life, light and love is the relentless drive to the divine. We have a choice between choosing to act consistent with the drive to the divine or choosing to act inconsistent with the drive to the divine. No one is more inherently evil than anyone else just as no one is more inherently good than anyone else. All of us contain the capacity for good and the capacity for evil. We have the choice for both at all times. When we consistently choose to live out of a recognition of the divinity of all things, we label this "goodness." Goodness sees the connectedness of all. When we consistently choose to live out of the illusion that nothing and no one around us is divine, we label this "evil." Evil sees the illusion that all is separate.

We all can develop evil patterns or habits in our lives. At some time in our lives, our natural drive to the divine becomes stunted, thwarted, diverted or perverted. When this happens, our drive to the divine turns in on itself and mutates into a drive to some base, material goal. Examples abound. A person who did not receive acceptance from his parents as an infant may spend his life engaging in sexual encounters without emotional intimacy in repeated attempts to fill the lack he experienced as a child. A person who is mesmerized by fear of survival may use all of her skills to spend all of her life acquiring material wealth to guard against the possibility of not having enough. A person who received abuse instead of affection (or abuse mixed with affection) may use alcohol or drugs to run from the pain, spiraling into addiction as a poor

> *Evil is habituated thoughts, actions, and words arising out of the illusion of separateness.*

and dangerous substitute for unmet basic human needs. Human suffering can feel like hell on earth, for both the person experiencing the pain and for people around the person.

Rather than waiting until we die to experience heaven or hell, we experience them right here in the material plane. Heaven and hell are not somewhere outside of us, they are within us. We are born with heaven, and during our childhood we start to import hell as well. Some of us are fortunate enough to import some heaven during that time, too. As adults, we choose moment by moment whether to export heaven or hell into our world. Most of us choose some mixture of heaven and hell to export, saving heavenly moments for our "loved ones," and exporting hellish moments to our "enemies." Whoever we define as family is usually given heavenly treatment. Whoever we define as dangerous to us, our family, or our lifestyle, we give hellish treatment. Everything and everyone is a part of us, so we end up exporting heaven and hell to ourselves. Ultimately, we choose from moment to moment what to export and to whom.

Evil is not outside of us. The potential for evil is within each of us. Evil is born by the choices we make. When we choose to act out of the illusion of separateness, we choose evil. When we choose to act in a manner that does not promote life, we choose evil. When we choose to act in a manner that does not promote light, we choose evil. When we choose to act in a manner that does not promote love, we choose evil.

Evil is not the absence of good, evil is acting on the illusion of separateness. Evil is created by humans, perpetuated by humans, and will be healed by humans. Evil is acting as if the person, place or thing in front of you is not divine. Evil arises out of human consciousness and will be transformed and transcended through human consciousness "re-membering" itself to divine consciousness.

How We Come to Evil Ways

FROM THE MOMENT OF CONCEPTION, WE ARE DIVINE. As we grow in the womb, we are nurtured and protected from all but the most violent physical harm. Even in the womb we are responsive to energies around us, both from the woman carrying us and the environments in which she finds herself. From the moment of conception, we are learning how the material world operates, openly receiving all patterns, both ones that promote life and

Chapter 2

health, and ones that promote death and disease. At conception, our energy field is a luminous globe of light, emitting energy without restriction, in all directions, like the sun. After leaving the womb, we continue to be receptive to all patterns of energy without any means to distinguish "good" from "bad," or healthy from unhealthy. Our primary teachers are the people around us, which for most of us are our parents and family. Most of our patterns we learn before we can even talk.

As spiritual beings coming into the material plane, we look to others in the material plane to learn how to navigate this world. We learn both transcendent patterns and wounded patterns, with the amount of each depending on the environments in which we find ourselves. Most parents and other caregivers truly love the children in their care and do their best to live patterns which are beneficial to the child. Every parent and caregiver I have spoken with wishes to provide a better childhood to the child in their care than they themselves had. Most of us do at least one step better. This incremental process contributes to the evolution of consciousness, giving our children a few less unhelpful patterns to overcome.

One pattern that most of us in the West learn is the idea that we are each individuals, separate from all around us. This pattern has both some utility and some limitations. The individuality pattern has utility to teach us agency. When we learn agency, we learn that we are responsible for the actions and thoughts arising from the body in which we have manifested in this lifetime. The primary limitation of the individuality pattern is that we can become mesmerized by the illusion of separateness and live our lives as if the illusion were real. It is true that we have a quality of individuality in our manifestation. It is also true that we have a quality of connectedness - being part of something bigger than ourselves - in our manifestation. People without a developed sense of individuality are not effective actors in the material world. People without a developed sense of connectedness wound others with their inflated sense of importance.

No one who acts in a way that wounds others does so without first learning that pattern from the environment around him or her. No one has willfully harmed another without first being taught the insignificance of others by the way he or she has been treated. In studies about the personalities of persons who repeatedly engage in behaviors that wound others, they begin practicing on

Chapter 2

small animals and over time transfer those wounding behaviors to other humans, particularly those vulnerable and available. Evil develops over time as a consistent choice to live out of the illusion of separateness rather than the truth of connectedness.

When we see behaviors or words that we might consider evil, we often ask "How could anyone do (or say) that?" We have the question turned around. The question needs to be turned back to ourselves and asked, "What are the conditions under which I might find myself doing that?" Then we need to spend our energies minimizing the conditions under which evil becomes a choice one would make.

For example, humans have struggled with the existence of poverty for ages. However, when it comes to poverty, public policy has focused on ending poverty. Focusing on ending poverty is looking at the incorrect end of the spectrum of human acquisition. Instead of working to eradicate human poverty, we need to focus on what

> *There is enough in this world for man's need, but not man's greed.*
>
> *- Mohandas K. Gandhi*

conditions promote human greed and how we can minimize the opportunities to make greedy choices. Poverty is not the problem, greed is the problem. Greed arises from the illusion of separateness creating a need to hoard material things at the expense of others who are doing without essential needs. The illusion of separateness brings people to act out of a lack of love for their fellow humans.

In our world today, evil is not the problem, lack of love is the problem. "Those people" are not the problem. We are the problem. Healing within brings healing without. Behind every evil act and word lies fear.

Fear is the Soil from which Evil Grows

FEAR ARISES IN HUMAN CONSCIOUSNESS directly out of the illusion of separateness. Fear is an individual reaction to a belief that we are separate from each other and the world around us. Fear breeds judgment, shame, and isolation. When fear spreads from individuals to a community, it becomes stigma. Fear arises in individuals when they believe that there is something more powerful than they are which threatens

> *One of the greatest diseases is to be nobody to anybody.*
>
> *- Mother Teresa*

Chapter 2

their existence. Fear is a basic survival emotion which creates a physiological response. This physiological response focuses all the individual's bodily resources into surviving the threat by fight, flight or freeze. As a basic survival response, fear prompts us to move toward individual survival without thought to collective survival. Firefighters are trained to transcend the individual fear response to maximize survival of others. We can train ourselves to transcend fear as well. Fear, as a base survival response, has served humans well during the evolution of consciousness, and it is time to evolve our consciousness beyond a fear response.

Fear is an habitual pattern of thinking and feeling that does not promote life, light and love. Fear has an unlimited appetite for human energy and has the capability to swallow our energy no matter how much we generate or bring into our lives. Imagine we could quantify and measure energy. Imagine further that the average human uses 100,000 units of energy in his or her lifetime. Fear can swallow a lifetime of energy without the person even noticing where it went. Even if a person were extraordinary and brought in 250,000 units of energy into her life, she could spend it all on fear without anything to show for it. Since fear is an habitual pattern, we can unlearn fear. Part of unlearning fear is to recognize it as an illusion. The other part of unlearning fear is to invest our energy in its opposite, love.

To see fear as the illusion it really is, practice going to scary places. Now, I am not suggesting you go to dangerous places, but go to places in your life that stretch your comfort level. Go talk to that mean uncle who nobody likes. Try talking to your partner or spouse about something that has become taboo in your relationship. Spend time with yourself in solitude. To begin, choose something that makes you slightly uncomfortable, not your biggest trauma. Then spend some time in it and be self-reflective: does being in the situation merit the fear I have felt about the situation? If so, is there a way I can shift the dynamic or shift the way I engage it? If not, where is the fear coming from? What does it feel, taste, sound, smell like? Can I relate those sensations to some other experience in my life? These sensations of fear may be triggered by the situation from an earlier trauma in your life which has not been fully resolved. Section II of this book contains

> *Essentially all healing is the release from fear.*
>
> *- A Course in Miracles*

exercises that help you to begin unlearning fear. What seems to be an overwhelming task quickly becomes manageable and rewarding. Fear is often too wide to go around and too tall to go over, but it is paper thin; so stepping right into it is the best choice for facing it and moving beyond.

A person living in a higher consciousness recognizes that there may be events that annihilate the body, but there is nothing that can annihilate the divine. People who recognize their divinity and the divinity of others recognize that nothing can threaten their divine essence.

Divinity is the Soil from which Love Grows

LOVE ARISES IN HUMAN CONSCIOUSNESS directly out of the reality of connectedness. Love is our legacy arising out of the divine essence of which we are made. Love breeds compassion, forgiveness, and communion. Love in action among groups of people is the divine. Love arises in individuals when they know that there is nothing that can diminish their divinity. Love is our

> *Goodness is habituated thoughts, actions, and words arising out of the truth of connectedness.*

birthright in the evolution of our consciousness. Love is a name we use for the drive to the divine.

The drive to the divine is the force that compels us to pursue happiness and growth. We encounter the drive to the divine when we experience "flow" and other unitive experiences. It is the force that gets us back up on our feet after we have been knocked down. It is the force that whispers to us to trust one more time after betrayal, the force that urges us to love one more time after heartbreak. The drive to the divine is relentless and unlimited.

This unlimited reservoir is the source of human creativity. At bottom, when we produce great art, great music, and great literature, we do not know from where it comes. Inspiration is truly being infused by the divine. Great works come from hard work, but not necessarily in the way we think. The hard work is getting out of the way to let the divine shine through unfiltered. The hard work may occur long before the inspired work comes through us, or it may occur as the inspired work is being birthed.

Our Legacy: The Inner Spark within the Sacred Heart

AS WE LIVE INTO OUR LEGACY AS PART OF THE DIVINE, we

Chapter 2

come to recognize that we are never separate from the divine. At all times, in all places, with every challenge, we are connected. We have within us an inner spark – a spark of the divine that cannot be extinguished. It is in everyone at all times. No matter how many thoughts, actions and choices one has made inconsistent with it, the spark is still present, deep within us ready to ignite and reconnect us with the divine.

This inner spark is located at the place where the vertical axis crosses the horizontal axis in our energetic field. Various religious traditions have recognized this space and given it a name. One tradition calls this the sacred heart and locates it in the energetic space behind our physical heart. This sacred heart is the resting place of our inner spark, connecting us to the divine at all times. In India, the Sanskrit term for this space is Guba - literally the cave of the heart. The sacred heart, as an access point to the divine, provides us all knowledge, all power, and all love.

Being a Divine Warrior means making conscious choices to live out of our connection to the divine. It means making the path to our sacred heart well traveled. It means turning from a life focused on fear and survival to a life focused on manifesting the divine in our world.

Additional Readings for Chapter 2:

1. Avalo, Hector (2005). *Fighting Words: The Origins of Religious Violence.* Amherst, NY: Prometheus Books. ISBN # 1-59102-284-3 www.prometheusbooks.com

   > Provides an extensively researched framework suggesting that religious violence is based on creating scarce spiritual resources, including access to the divine, sacred space, and salvation.

2. Goldberg, C. (1996). *Speaking with the Devil: Exploring Senseless Acts of Evil.* New York, Penguin Books. www.penguin.com

   > Presents a logical progression of how an individual might move into patterns of actions that harm others.

3. Jung, Carl Gustav (1995) *Jung on Evil* (selected and introduced by Murray Stein). Princeton, NJ: Princeton University Press. ISBN # 0-691-026-17-3 pup.princeton.edu

   > An excellent collection of writings by Jung on the topic of evil.

4. Walsh, Michael (2003). *Warriors of the Lord: The Military Orders of Christendom.* Grand Rapids, MI: Eerdmans. ISBN # 0-8028-2109-X www.eerdmans.com

   > A narrative history amply illustrated of how Christianity came to embrace warfare as a "sacred" activity and the early days of waging war for the cause of religion.

Chapter 3

Divine Warriors

AS HUMANS, OUR CONSCIOUSNESS HAS EVOLVED to the place where it is the bridge between the spiritual and material planes. Our collective responsibility is to manifest the divine in the material plane. During phase 2 and phase 3 of the evolution of consciousness, from the time we separated from unitive consciousness to now, we have created a great deal of trauma in the world. Much of this trauma continues to pollute our collective consciousness. Not only are we collectively responsible for the trauma, we are collectively responsible for the healing of it.

Axis Mundi

MANY INDIGENOUS TRADITIONS have a concept of the cosmic tree, with the branches representing the heavens, the trunk representing the world humans populate and the roots representing the underworld. One label used for this concept is axis mundi: the center pole around which the world or cosmos revolves. Religions have established sacred sites based on claims of the world beginning at, or centering around, the site selected, including trees (the banyan or bodhi in India), mountains (Mount Kailash in Tibet, Mount Shasta in California), and locations (for example, Mecca and Jerusalem). For Christians, the symbol of the cross is where heaven and earth meet, representing God in human form.

In reality, humans are the axis mundi: humans are the part of creation that traverses both the material realm and the spiritual realm. Humans are the center pole around which the cosmos revolves. Our collective task on earth is to bridge the gap in consciousness we have created between heaven and earth. Our energetic bodies are comprised of seven major energy vortexes aligned vertically from our perineum (between our legs) to our crown. The lower three major vortexes are associated with material concerns, including

Chapter 3

safety, procreation, and belongingness. The higher three major energy vortexes are associated with spiritual concerns, including the power of choice, intuition, and connection to the divine. In the middle is the major energy vortex located at the heart. If we stand with our arms outstretched to each side, parallel to the floor, this major energy vortex is roughly in line with our outstretched arms. We each have within us the marriage of the spiritual world and the material world - the marriage of heaven and earth. Our collective purpose on this planet is to balance the material and the spiritual – to manifest the divine in the material world. In doing so, we complete the circle of consciousness returning to the divine consciousness out of which everything arises.

> *I, God, became [human] and humanity became God through the union of my divine nature with your human nature. This greatness is given to every person in general....*
>
> *- Catherine of Siena*

Our collective idea of reality that we have currently manifested is focused on material concerns. In the axis mundi, this would be the horizontal line, what we could call "logos," a

Greek word from which comes the English word "logic." Humans as material beings focus on reasoning and their five senses to navigate the world. Western science is built on logos, with theories and hypotheses only advanced if they are agreed upon by others or supported by events observable by more than one person.

The spiritual world is focused on our relationship to the divine. In the axis mundi, this would be the vertical line, what we could call "agios," the Greek word from which comes the English word "holy." The vertical line connects us to that which is greater than us. In the world we have currently created, we have focused primarily on logos, resulting in advances in technology and scientific knowledge. Logos can be used to explain how something works the way it does, but does nothing to explain why something works the way it does. We use logos to explain how a seed germinates, but we need agios to explain why a seed germinates. We have grown out of balance by focusing on logos and neglecting agios. Logos helps us navigate the world; agios helps us bring meaning to our lives. Agios gives us the drive toward the divine, the drive toward light, life, and love.

Chapter 3

Closing the Gap

OUR COLLECTIVE PURPOSE - to manifest the divine in the material world - has been hampered by the ways we have traumatized each other over the history of humankind. While each of us has been wounded, each of us also has a drive to the divine. Out of the drive to the divine, we can choose a path of healing. The healing path first minimizes the trauma we inflict on others in our life and then begins to heal the traumas we have endured. Once we have begun to heal ourselves, we can then begin to help others heal their traumas. Living in consciousness which recognizes the divine in all creation begins to close the gap. We can bring the divine into the material world by the daily choices we make. As we choose to think, act and speak out of a choice toward light, life and love, we choose the divine. As our choices for light, life, and love become more and more prominent in our lives, the divine is born into this world though our consciousness. When we begin to see the goodness in ourselves, we think, act and speak with more goodness. When we begin to see the goodness in others, they begin to think, act and speak with more goodness.

Many of us are at war with ourselves. Many of us are at

war within ourselves. The violence we see, hear and read about is only a manifestation of the greater battle within our psyches. As we struggle in this internal battle, our greatest weapon as well as our greatest weakness is choice. Choice is what can move us toward the divine and choice is what can keep us separated from the divine. Americans in particular value freedom principally because it offers choice – the power to choose. In this moment, the most powerful force a human has at her or his disposal is the power of choice. Even when the power of choice of behavior is taken from us, we still have the power of choice with our attitude and view of life. Viktor Frankl shared this truth in his compelling story of choosing to love in the midst of being imprisoned in a concentration camp.

> *Between stimulus and response there is a space. In that space is our power to choose our response. In our response lies our growth and our freedom.*
>
> *- Viktor Frankl*

Many of us are losing this war with ourselves because we have lost sight of the battlefield. The battlefield is not "out there" in the world – the battlefield is inside us. As long as we project

Chapter 3

the battlefield outside of ourselves, we will never be victorious. Peace within is achieved through attention to and diligent work on ourselves. Peace within breeds peace without. Peace within, victory in the battle for our souls, is achieved by becoming a divine warrior.

Living in the Trinity

A DIVINE WARRIOR IS ONE WHO FINDS A BALANCE inside the trinity of relationships: relationship with self; relationship with other; relationship with the divine. Attending to only one of these three creates imbalance. Attending to two of these three creates imbalance. Only when our life is focused on developing all three relationships will we find balance. Focusing only on the relationship with self breeds egoism. Focusing only on the relationship with other breeds resentment when one's needs are not met. Focusing only on the relationship with the divine breeds elitism, a sense that we are somehow better than others because we have a special relationship to the divine. Because all that exists is part of the divine, all of the relationships are in essence aspects of our relationship with the divine.

Each of these relationships has a core value from which is

derived a central process. Our values provide us the lens through which we view the world. Our values drive the choices we make in our thoughts, actions and speech. A central process is the path we take to live out of the values we have chosen. Divine warriors do not just have "stated" values and their values are not simply "held;" divine warriors live their values in every moment. From moment to moment, divine warriors make choices based on their core values until their thinking, acting and speaking arises spontaneously from their core values. As this discipline is applied, it produces patterns of thinking, acting and speaking that manifest the divine in this world. In this way, divine warriors assist in the evolution of consciousness to "re-member" themselves and others to the divine.

Trinity of relationships	Value	Central Process
Relationship with self	Living-Authentic	Integration
Relationship with other	Living-Kindness	Compassion
Relationship with divine	Living-Surrender	Gratitude

Relationship with Self

AN ESSENTIAL COMPONENT OF BECOMING a divine warrior is

Chapter 3

to develop a relationship with oneself. Many of us have unresolved issues of self worth, forgetting we always and in every moment have the unquenchable inner spark of the divine. Our self worth does not come from who we are in the world, or what we have accomplished, or what we have acquired. Our self worth is inherent – it has always existed and will always exist no matter what we do or say to try to extinguish it. Every life has value. Every human comes into the world with the essence of the divine and brings to this material existence purpose, skills and challenges.

> *A child of the divine grows up to be the divine.*

Our collective purpose is to manifest the divine in this world. Each of us has an individual purpose, a reason for being born. As divine warriors, it is our responsibility to delve deep into ourselves to uncover our individual purpose for being here. Some of us remember clearly what we were born into this world to do. Some of us take nearly our whole life to rediscover this individual purpose. There is an abundance of techniques and methods for discovering your divine purpose. Meditative and contemplative practices, which teach self-reflection, are efficient vehicles for gaining clarity about our individual purpose. There is no one right way to be self reflective, each of us must find our own individual right way. When we follow a path into activities in which we lose all sense of time – that which we get lost in – we are on the trail to our true purpose.

> *Follow your bliss.*
> *- Joseph Campbell*

Each of us brings into this world a set of skills which are aligned with our individual purpose. These skills are like seeds, waiting to germinate when the conditions are right, growing into abilities that allow us to manifest our individual purpose in the world. No skill set is the same, and all skill sets are sufficient unto themselves for the work at hand. In addition to the skills we have developed in our lives, there are other skill seeds available to us waiting to germinate and develop. The breadth and depth of these skill seeds are beyond our wildest dreams.

Each of us brings into this world a set of challenges which are also aligned with our individual purpose. These challenges can be viewed as patterns arising from past traumas. These patterns are associated with incomplete attempts to fully manifest the divine in the material world. These challenges provide us an opportunity

Chapter 3

to heal collective trauma. At the same time, these challenges carry the risk of diverting us from our individual purpose. No one is given challenges too large to bear. A person with great challenges is given great skills. Some of us are still being pulled under by the force of our challenges because we have not yet completed the circle in the divine game. Persons who have been pulled under by their challenges can turn tragedy into triumph by being provided the conditions that remind them of their divine essence and allow for reconnection to the divine. Addictions of all sorts arise from being swept under by our challenges, and all effective addiction treatments have at their core a reconnection to divine source. An addiction is nothing more than a weak substitute for the energy available to us from the divine. For example, drowning our pain in substance use is a weak substitute for the healing power of recognizing our own divine essence.

As we confront and overcome our challenges, the struggle becomes our strength – the same process holds true for our spiritual muscles as well as our physical muscles. In this way, we turn tragedy into triumph. This is the process of transformation we are called to do in this material world.

The core value of relationship with self is living-authentic, living into being the same outside as inside. The core process to live into this value is integration, where who we are on the inside, with all our purpose, skills and challenges, becomes who we are on the outside. As our recognition of our divine essence grows, we become less and less interested in what other people think of us. We derive our identity not from the approval of others, but from the divine essence within us. As we become less interested in what other people think of us, we are able to live more and more from the inside out, understanding that we are a work in progress among many other works in progress. Integrating our outward self with the inward self, we become one with ourselves, no longer needing to expend energy managing how we are perceived, instead investing that energy on who we are becoming in the fullness of our manifestation of the divine.

> *Be the change you wish to see in the world.*
>
> *- Mohandas K. Gandhi*

My process of living-authentic began in earnest in the summer of 1997. I had made a mess of my life. I was unhappy to the point of contemplating suicide. I recognized that I had lived my life up to that point by doing what I thought would gain the approval of other people in my life. At the lowest point of my life, I decided to continue living, and decided that the only way I wanted to live was to be true to myself without concern about the approval of others. I made a choice for the first time to follow my inner guidance rather than follow my idea of what would lead to other people's approval of me. Following this path was very difficult at first, and it took risking everything I held dear in my life. As I grew to value myself and my divine essence, it became easier and easier to follow the path of living-authentic. As who we are inside becomes more and more who we are outside, we integrate our fractured life into a whole, which is the essence of healing.

Included in the process of integration is the gift we give ourselves of self forgiveness. Also included in the process of integration is a consistent focus toward positive thoughts, actions, and speech. Self forgiveness and investing in positive energy are key elements of the process of healing ourselves.

Relationship with Other

AN ESSENTIAL COMPONENT OF BECOMING a divine warrior

is to develop a relationship with other. As humans, our biggest challenge in all the categories of other is the category of other humans. Our judgment of other humans is directly related to the extent to which we recognize the divine within ourselves. If we truly have come to recognize the divine within ourselves, then we recognize the divine in others. If we judge others and their paths, we have lost sight of the divine within ourselves. In this way, Jesus' statement, "Love your neighbor as yourself" is not a command to which we are to aspire, but a law of human nature: "You will love your neighbor to the extent to which you love yourself." As we attend to our relationship with self, our living-authentic bears fruit as well in our relationship with other, where the core value is living-kindness and the core process is compassion.

The core value of living-kindness means that as we recognize the divine within us, we recognize the divine in others. All of creation shares the same essence of the divine – in this way we are all of the same kind. The worth of others does not come from who they are in the world, or what they have accomplished, or what they have acquired. Their worth

> *I am you in another form.*

is inherent – it has always existed and will always exist no matter what we do or say to try to extinguish it. Every life has value. Every human comes into the world with the essence of the divine and brings to this material existence purpose, skills and challenges.

My process of living-kindness also began in the summer of 1997. Up to that point in my life, I had judged the actions and speech of others with little regard for the path they had traveled. I was eaten up with self judgment, which I projected out to others. Just as living-authentic requires self forgiveness, living-kindness requires forgiving others. I began to see that others are doing the best they can and the part they play in my life is to provide me opportunities for growth. My perception of the world moved from seeing myself as a victim to seeing myself as an active participant in how my life unfolds.

Included in the central process of compassion is recognizing the divine in others, which makes respecting them natural. In living-kindness, we attend to creating safe and sacred space for the purpose, skills and challenges of others to unfold and transform. Forgiveness is a discipline of the divine warrior, who recognizes that we are in each other's lives to provide opportunities to reawaken to the divine. The core process of compassion is a process of healing each other.

Relationship with Divine

AN ESSENTIAL COMPONENT OF BECOMING a divine warrior is to develop a relationship with the divine. This relationship focus assists us in finding our place among all that is. A relationship with the divine reminds us that our problems are not enormous, not intractable, and not insurmountable. It reminds us that we have the entire universe as our resource. From the perspective of infinity and eternity, any situation we face is seen for what it is: infinitesimal and insignificant. The relationship with the divine keeps a divine warrior from becoming mired in the minutiae of life. It allows a divine warrior to gain a perspective broader and deeper than an individual life, rising above the fray to see the lay of the land with eagle's eyes.

The core value for the relationship with the divine is living surrender. Once a divine warrior becomes "re-membered" to the divine, we recognize that our life is not our own, and it was but an illusion that it ever was. Our value becomes surrendering to our divine purpose, honing our divine skills, and transforming our

Chapter 3

divine challenges.

The process of living-surrender also began for me in the summer of 1997. With my life in shambles, I pledged the remainder of my life to serve the divine. In real and clear terms, I died to my self and turned over the controls of my life to the divine. I accepted the core value of living-surrender in my life.

> *All that I am in this moment*
> *All that I have been*
> *All that I will be*
>
> *O Spirit, I surrender to you.*
>
> *This life, this year,*
> *This week, this day,*
> *This hour, this moment.*

The central process to manifest this core value of living-surrender is gratitude. Discarding the illusion of separateness brings us back to an awareness of the abundance surrounding us at all times and in all places. A natural response to abundance is gratitude. As we grow in gratitude, service becomes central to our existence, and the opportunity for service to the divine is everywhere and "everywhen." Living in a relationship of trust of the divine breeds gratitude.

Living in the trinity of relationships brings us to a center point where we hold three truths simultaneously as we work to manifest the divine in the material plane: we are indispensable; we are interchangeable; we are insignificant. In our relationship with self we learn that it is only our choice of thoughts, actions and speech that manifests the divine in this world, making us indispensable. In our relationship with other we learn that how we engage and support others manifests the divine in this world, making us interchangeable. In our relationship with the divine we learn that none of our choices is irreversible in completing the evolution of consciousness, making us insignificant. We all are, in every moment, indispensable, interchangeable, and insignificant. As the axis mundi, our collective purpose is to live into manifesting the divine in all our relationships. As the axis mundi we become divine warriors by choosing the divine in our thoughts, actions and speech. Divine warriors choose the path of healing. We are responsible for closing the gap we have created between heaven and earth, between the divine and the material.

CHAPTER 3

ADDITIONAL RESOURCES FOR CHAPTER 3:

1.   Campbell, Joseph (1972). *The Hero with a Thousand Faces.* Princeton, NJ: Princeton University Press. ISBN # 978-0691017846 pup.princeton.edu

> The path of the divine warrior has many parallels with the hero's journey described by Joseph Campbell.

2.   Catherine of Siena (1980). *The Dialogue* (translated by Suzanne Noffke). New York: Paulist Press. ISBN # 0-8091-2233-2 www.paulistpress.com

> An account by a fourteenth century Catholic mystic containing her vision as transmitted directly from the divine.

3.   Frankl, Viktor (1997). *Man's Search for Meaning: An Introduction to Logotherapy* (Rev. Ed.). New York: Pocket. ISBN # 0-671-02337-3 www.simonsays.com

> Frankl provides an inspiring picture of the triumph of human spirit and love over hateful actions toward others.

4.   Ramachandra Rao, Saligrama Krishna (1979). *Jivanmukti in Advaita.* Bangalore, India: IBH Prakashana for the Sankara Educational Trust.

> Jivanmukti is a term used in Hindu philosophy which

translates as "living liberation," one who is still living in the world and is liberated from the illusion of reality ("Maya"). This Hindu concept parallels the concept of divine warrior presented in this book.

5.   Shantideva (2003). *The Way of the Bodhisattva: A Translation of the Bodhicharyavatara.* Boston: Shambhala. ISBN # 978-1590300572. www.shambhala.com

Bodhisattva is a term used in Buddhist philosophy which translates as "enlightened being." This Buddhist concept parallels the concept of divine warrior presented in this book.

Chapter 3

The following is a list of statements I have gathered that help guide me in my path. I call it my Code. You are welcome to adopt it in its entirety, adopt parts of it, or not use it at all. Creating your own code gives you a wonderful reminder of the values you are living.

A Code for a Divine Warrior

1. The divine exists within you and cannot be extinguished.
2. The divine exists within each and every person and cannot be extinguished.
3. The divine exists within all creation and cannot be extinguished.
4. Nothing and no one is perfect, and everything and everyone is divine.
5. Every moment offers a choice.
6. Fear is of the mind, courage is of the heart.
7. The threat from within is greater than the threat from without.
8. Balance time with others and solitude.
9. Everyone is a teacher and not everyone is a student.
10. It does not matter what "they do to you." What matters is what you do with what "they do to you."
11. Discard self-pity. It is a useless weapon for a warrior.
12. Do not say anything about someone that you are unwilling to say to his or her face.

CHAPTER 4

HEALING OURSELVES

THE PATH OF A DIVINE WARRIOR is a path of healing. The path has the same effect as dropping a pebble into a calm pool of water. First, the pebble displaces water exactly where it enters: a divine warrior begins the healing path working on her or his own wounds, going deep into her or his core to find divine essence. The second effect of the pebble is a ripple which encompasses and surrounds the initial point of impact: a divine warrior develops skills to hold the space for others to heal. The third ripple expands outward reaching a wider scope of influence: a divine warrior continues on the healing path working in every moment in the world at large to manifest the divine.

Healing ourselves means "re-membering" ourselves to the divine. Holding on to our wounds drags us down into limitations. Healing our wounds raises us up into our potential.

Finding our Spiritual Essence

WE ARE NOT OUR BODY. Our bodies are instruments gifted to us for our use in navigating the world. Every body is different in size, shape and appearance, and every body is the same in having incredible potential for growth and healing. Our bodies are the most amazing tools we will ever encounter. Any limitations of our bodies that we perceive are nothing more than limitations of our perceptions of them.

If we spend energy focusing on the limitations or shortcomings of our bodies, we are feeding energy into those perceptions and those limitations will manifest. There are people who spend their whole lives trying to get their body to appear perfect and it never does. There are people who spend their energy fearing a certain disease, and that disease often manifests.

If we spend energy focusing on the amazing properties

and potentials of our bodies, we are feeding energy into those perceptions and those potentials will manifest. Name a favorite athlete and we will find that she or he has invested a vast amount of time and energy into the potential of her or his body as an instrument of achievement in that sport.

The most beautiful aspect of this instrument we call a body is its potential for change. Genetics are nothing more than invitations to live into a certain pattern. Our environment, including how we invest our energy, determines whether the invitation contained in our genes is accepted. The way we care for this instrument determines how well it serves us. The body's potential for change means that we can choose at any moment to change the way we treat our body and it will respond positively. Longstanding patterns of mistreatment take concerted time and effort to change with attention on all aspects of our energetic field: spiritual; mental; emotional; and physical.

We are not our emotions. Our emotions are feedback to tell us whether we are on our path or off our path. Positive emotions provide feedback that we are on our path. Negative emotions provide feedback that we are off our path. Emotions are less essential for human survival and the evolution of human consciousness than they were in the past. No emotion, no matter how strong, lasts indefinitely, even though it can feel indefinite while we are in the middle of it. Emotions dissipate when we breathe into them and embrace them. Emotions linger and become part of a pattern of response when we fear them or try to push them away. People who have achieved greatness have learned to master their emotions and harness them to advance their vision.

We are not our thoughts. Our thoughts are invitations of where to invest our energy. When we invest our energy in a thought, more thoughts of a similar vibration are attracted to the thought we have energized, just as metal filings are attracted to a magnet. In every moment, each one of us has unlimited choices in the thoughts in which we choose to invest. Every moment we can make a different choice, no matter how many times we have made the same choice before. Perhaps I have always thought that a certain group of people is not to be trusted. At any moment, I can choose to test that pattern of thought and experiment in trusting a member of that group of people. The evidence I receive back can be used to inform my choice of thoughts about trustworthiness. No matter how much I try, I will never have all the data on trustworthiness for all the people whom I consider to be members of that group. While it is accurate to perceive that we have created a world where not everyone is trustworthy, there is no evidence that any one group we could name is more trustworthy than any other. Which thoughts are more beneficial to energize, the thoughts that focus on the few people we encounter who are untrustworthy, or the thoughts that focus on the people we encounter who are trustworthy? The first choice invests our energy in the world as we have currently imagined it into being and the second choice invests our energy into the divine potential waiting to be manifested.

When we focus too much of our energy on the way our body looks, or the emotion moving through us, or the thoughts inviting us to distraction, we become mired in the minutiae. Becoming mired in the minutiae leads us away from the path of a divine warrior into whirlpools of unproductive energy. These whirlpools feed on themselves and drag us down into our limitations arising from our wounds.

Being Human Means Being Wounded

TO LIVE LIFE IS TO EXPERIMENT with finding truth. It is what we are all here for. If we do not experiment, we are moving through the world dead. Most of us live life as a series of small experiments so that if the experiment fails, there are small consequences. Some of us live life with big experiments, resulting in big successes or big failures. Whether we experiment big or experiment small, none of us always succeeds. Because we do not live our lives in a vacuum, but live our lives in relation to the world around us, including other humans, our failures often affect other humans. We call these failures "mistakes" and we call the effect the mistakes have on others "wounds." Our experiments with living, when not successful, are mistakes that can wound other humans. People who experiment without regard to the effect on other humans we call reckless or thoughtless, and people living this way can leave plenty of wounds in their paths. Most of us, though, learn from both the failures and successes of our experiments and adjust our next experiment based on the things we have learned. As divine warriors, our first task in healing

> *My imperfections and failures are as much a blessing from God as my successes and my talents, and I lay them both at [God's] feet.*
>
> *- Mohandas K. Gandhi*

ourselves is to recognize that failures are nothing to fear, they are a necessary part of being in the material plane and growing toward our divine legacy. It is estimated that young children attempt to stand on two feet over 300 times before they succeed. Any great accomplishment takes extraordinary practice as the person moves closer and closer to the vision she or he holds for success.

Releasing our fear of failure to embrace mistakes takes the following steps:

#1 Recognize that while in this material world, we will be imperfect.

#2 Realize that the things we identify as "mistakes" are opportunities to learn and grow.

#3 Realize that we have within us and around us all the resources we need to make choices that promote love, light and life in the world.

#4 Realize that everyone else is in the same process and has the same internal resources to learn from his or her life experiences and our role is to support each other in our paths of healing.

Woundedness is pervasive in our world and it can be categorized in many ways. One way to categorize woundedness that might be useful is to say there is "local" woundedness and "nonlocal" woundedness. Local woundedness is more familiar to us. Local woundedness is a threat or harm to our physical, mental, emotional or spiritual being in this lifetime. It is what we would call personal: it happens in such a way that you perceive it as happening to your individual being or self. Local woundedness includes all of the victim statuses we have come to recognize. Local woundedness includes the physical wounds, verbal wounds (including negative self talk), emotional wounds, and spiritual limitations we experience. Local woundedness becomes part of our life story, and sometimes we can get caught up in an eddy of energy that keeps us stuck in our story. Healing the wounds from your life story is essential for healing the world.

Nonlocal woundedness is the collection of unhealed human wounds accumulated since the first awakening of human consciousness. I believe that when people talk about, or feel they are accessing "past lives," they are accessing nonlocal wounds. It is not the same soul living in a body today that occupied a body 100 years ago, it is a soul incarnate today accessing a collection of memories and wounds that occurred in the collective past of humankind. For example, we may have never experienced dying in a natural disaster, but some of us may be able to tap into the collective experience of humans in the past who have died in a natural disaster. In this sense, the wound did not happen to this particular human being (and therefore is not local woundedness); the wound happened to a soul previously incarnated in the human family. Because a wound is nonlocal does not mean it has no energetic charge or has no need of healing. Nonlocal wounds can be as powerful in our energy field as a local wound, and nonlocal wounds are as important to heal as local wounds.

Some of us get caught up in the story of the wounding experience rather than focusing on the healing. Hearing the story of a wounding is an important part of healing, but it is not the end of the process - the person experiencing the wound must be willing to transform the wound and move on with his or her life. As divine warriors, we are responsible for supporting a person in his or her healing process by hearing the story and creating sacred space for healing and transformation. We can transform our own wounds by focusing on our spiritual essence and recognizing that all of our experiences can provide us opportunities for growth.

Transforming Our Wounds

NO MATTER THE CIRCUMSTANCES in which we were born, no matter the conditions under which we were raised, no matter the life we have lived up to this moment, we can each feed the seed of the divine within us and begin the process of transformation. It is not an easy path. It is a path that holds both suffering and sacrifice, as well as a path that holds celebration and connectedness. Once we begin this path, we turn away from our limiting sense of being only material beings. As we continue along the transformational path, we start seeing longer and longer glimpses of the divine. I cannot promise that suffering will leave us completely in this lifetime. Life in the material plane is not designed to be always and completely comfortable. Great accomplishments require great sacrifice. But this path of healing does provide a sense of completeness, connection, and purpose missing for many of us today.

None of us either earns or deserves the status into which we are born. Whether rich or poor, disabled or fully able, male or female, no matter what ethnicity, sexual orientation, national origin or creed, the statuses we take on at birth are not earned. These statuses are a gift we can call an accident of birth. No matter what

Chapter 4

accident of birth we are gifted, we need each of us to transform our material circumstances and manifest the divine in this material plane. What is needed in each life is a death to circumstances and a rebirth to divine purpose. If we were born to poverty and violence, we need transformation to abundance and peace. If we were born to wealth and privilege, we need transformation to seeing the interconnectedness of our existence. If we have lived a life of using and abusing others, we need transformation to recognizing the divine in others. If we have lived a life of being victimized, we need transformation to recognizing the divine in ourselves. Whatever our unique circumstances of life, we have the opportunity to manifest the divine by transforming our limitations.

> *I can be changed by what happens to me. I refuse to be reduced by it.*
>
> *- Maya Angelou*

No path is inherently more difficult than another in the transformation process. Comparing your path to others is a distraction from the transformational path of healing. Some of us see others with more resources and wish that we had their path. We see it from our perspective as "easy," or at least "easier." Having more resources can be a difficult path to the divine, because reliance on material possessions must be transcended. Some well-intentioned people view others with fewer resources as having a more "difficult" path. This is also a distraction from the transformational path of healing, as it breeds pity and "helping behavior" that diverts the helpers from attending to their wounds and focusing on their need for healing.

SELF FORGIVENESS

BEING IN THE MATERIAL PLANE means being faced with, and buffeted by, forces which are not healthy to our development and some are clearly destructive and malicious. In our world today people do things to other people which cause unintentional harm. There are also people who do things to other people with a malevolent intent to harm. In order to heal and move to a place of wholeness, we first need to limit the harm being done by removing ourselves from a harmful situation or reducing the harm being committed. Next, we need to make an accurate attribution of responsibility. This attribution comes in two parts. First, responsibility needs to be accurately attributed to the person causing the harm, whether intentional or not. In the process of healing by

Chapter 4

the person harmed, this is what could be called the "victim stage:" a recognition that something was done to us that was harmful and it was at the hands of someone else. Many of us who are healing get stuck in this stage. Some of us who do not even get to this stage often engage in a process that has come to be known as "blaming the victim," which is inaccurately attributing the responsibility for the harm to the person being harmed. This inaccurate and unhelpful process of blaming the victim gets confused with the next step of healing, which is taking responsibility for the part we played in the harmful dynamic.

Some victims, when the situation or experience is examined, have no responsibility in the harmful dynamic. For example, children who are abused by their caregivers are not responsible for the harmful experience because they are not old enough to be independent actors in the dynamic. On the other hand, most adults who experience relationship wounds even as victims share at least a fraction of the responsibility for the harmful dynamic in which they found themselves. Part of

> *No one can make you feel inferior without your consent.*
>
> *-Eleanor Roosevelt*

healing is taking the next step: reflecting on what about us provided an opening for the harm to occur. Did we trust too much? Did we expose our vulnerabilities to the wrong type of person? Did we put up with being treated poorly? For example, when we work with domestic violence victims we seek to empower them to leave the abuser. Staying with the abuser, while often understandable from the victim's perspective, still provides an opportunity for more abuse. Creating a safety plan becomes a part that the victim can play in reducing or stopping the abuse, even if the victim does not feel safe enough to leave the abuser.

Once we have come to see our part (even if it is a fractional part) in the harm occurring, then one of the most difficult steps comes next: forgiving ourselves. Forgiving ourselves comes when we get to the place where we acknowledge and truly believe that we did the best we could during the experience given who we were at that time. We learn to not measure our actions on what we know now or who we are now, but on what we knew then and who we were then. Once we get to the place of believing we did the best we could at the time, then we are on the path to forgiving ourselves and can choose to forgive the other participants in the wounding.

Chapter 4

Forgiving the person wounding us requires healing to a place where we have performed alchemy on the harm, transforming something unwanted into a celebrated part of who we are and recognizing that we would not have grown into the fullness of who we have become without those events. This is not to say that the wound was enjoyable at the time or that the person who committed the acts is absolved of responsibility, but it is to say that the wound no longer has power over us. We have successfully turned the wound into a strength.

Exhaling our Limitations, Inhaling our Potentials

IF WE CONTINUE TO BREATHE, we continue to live. If we continue to heal, we continue to grow. Self forgiveness is an essential element for healing – it helps us to move our wounds and self judgment out of our energetic system. When we heal, we exhale our limitations. As we begin

> *The blessing is next to the wound.*
> *- African saying*

to let go of and release the wounds that bind us to our limitations, we free up more energy to invest in our potentials. The other essential element for healing is inhaling: drawing in divine energy

Divine Warrior Training

to live into our potential. We cannot fully breathe when we only exhale or when we only inhale. Breathing requires both exhaling and inhaling. Healing requires both exhaling and inhaling.

For healing, inhaling means finding connection to the divine and drawing the divine into our energetic system. Each of us must find our own unique access to the divine. It is the responsibility of each of us to find our inhalation stations – those places and circumstances that fill us up with the divine. For some, it might be church, synagogue or mosque. For some, it might be nature. For some, it might be creative endeavors. For some, it might be solitude. For some, it might be community. For some, it might be inspirational books or music. Finding the places and circumstances where we can inhale divine energy is essential for healing.

For maximum healing, our inhalation stations need to be all around us and integrated into our daily lives. We find them in things we have done since childhood, in the things we have mastered, and in the things in which we lose ourselves. Some of the inhalation stations for me are walking, mowing the lawn, buying fruits and vegetables, washing dishes, and being in nature. Walking and mowing the lawn are activities I have enjoyed since

Chapter 4

childhood. In my teens, I became a produce manager for a small local grocery, so buying fruits and vegetables is a skill I have mastered. Washing dishes is a daily activity that not only gives me a sense of accomplishment, it gives me a sense of contributing to the household, the people with whom I share space. Being in nature puts my individual thoughts, emotions and challenges back into proper perspective, reminding me that I am part of something bigger and I do not have to do everything.

Finding our inhalation stations provides us the fuel for healing, repatterning our lives to release our limitations and draw in our potentials. In this way, we "re-member" ourselves to the divine, and we come to a place where we "re-cognize" ourselves as divine. As we heal and "re-cognize" the divine within us, we are able to exhale divine energy as well.

> *The kingdom of God is within you.*
>
> *- Jesus of Nazareth*

Comfort as Holding our Healing Breath

MANY OF US HAVE BECOME ADDICTED TO COMFORT. We pursue comfort at great expense: financial expense to ourselves, environmental expense to the planet, economic justice expense to poor people in resource-rich parts of the world, and spiritual expense to ourselves. When we seek comfort at the expense of healing, we are clinging to the wounds that limit us.

Comfort is not the ultimate goal in being alive – healing is. Healing is not always comfortable, and sometimes resting is a necessary part of healing. However, resting and comfort are not the same. Life is not always comfortable. Loved ones get sick. Loved ones die. We make choices that impact each others' lives. None of us is guaranteed a life of comfort, no matter who we are. Life is not necessarily hard, and it is certainly not easy. Yes, there are difficult parts of living, and it is natural and necessary for us to seek rest at times. But we have made life difficult for the wrong reasons: we have made life hard in the way we wound each other; in the way we withhold basic survival needs from each other; in the way we judge each other. These unnecessary wounds have left us striving for the basic necessities of life, scurrying about trying to make ends meet, and then needing to rest from the push to survive and acquire. Survival and acquisition then feed the need for more material things and the need for more comfort, all the while neglecting our need for healing. We can obsess about material survival in the midst

Chapter 4

of material abundance, or we can turn our faces back to healing ourselves, healing others, and healing the world around us. Divine warriors can heal ourselves by exhaling our limitations and inhaling our potentials, and we can heal ourselves by finding for ourselves, and creating for others, safe places to rest and "re-member" us to the divine. In this way we move into our relationship with self through living-authentic.

> *A slogan for healing ourselves:*
> ## *Aspire to Authenticity*

Additional Readings for Chapter 4:

1. Ardagh, Arjuna (2005). *The Translucent Revolution: How People Just Like You Are Waking Up and Changing the World*. Novato, CA: New World Library. ISBN # 1-57731-468-9
www.newworldlibrary.com

> This book provides a collection of stories and processes illustrating that people from all walks of life and stations are finding their own unique path to healing and connection to the divine.

2. Csikszentmihalyi, Mihaly. (1993). *Flow: The Psychology of Optimal Experience*. New York, Perennial. ISBN # 978-0060920432
www.harpercollins.com

> For more information about those times when we lose our sense of individual self, this book provides a psychological framework for these experiences, which the author calls "flow."

3. Gandhi, M.K. (1957). *An Autobiography: The Story of My Experiments with Truth*. Boston: Beacon Press. ISBN # 0-8070-5909-9
www.beacon.org

> A rich and inspiring recounting in his own words of Gandhi's early life before he became a public figure.

4. Kabat-Zinn, Jon (1994). *Wherever You Go There You Are*. New York: Hyperion. ISBN # 0-7868-8070-8
www.hyperionbooks.com

CHAPTER 4

> A beautiful collection of short essays on living in the moment, this book is a wonderful daily companion on the path of healing.

5.   Levine, Peter A. (1997). *Waking the Tiger: Healing Trauma.* Berkeley, CA: North Atlantic Books. www.northatlanticbooks.com

> For readers who want more specific but not too technical information about our human reaction to stress and danger, this book provides useful information for understanding trauma and the path of healing.

6.   Peck, M. Scott (2003). *The Road Less Traveled, 25th Anniversary Edition: A New Psychology of Love, Traditional Values and Spiritual Growth.* New York: Touchstone. ISBN # 978-0743243155 www.simonsays.com

> This book is a classic in the field of spiritual growth and taking one's life into one's own hands. It played an important part in my early spiritual and personal development.

7.   Teasdale, Wayne (2004). *The Mystic Hours: A Daybook of Interspiritual Wisdom & Devotion.* Novato, CA: New World Library. ISBN # 1-57731-472-7 www.newworldlibrary.com

> The title of this book adequately describes this gem!

CHAPTER 5

HEALING OTHERS

AS WE BEGIN TO HEAL OURSELVES, we learn the importance of safe space for healing. The more we are able to create safe space for ourselves, the more we are able to create safe space for others. Healing others means "re-membering" them to the divine. When we impose our idea of who or what someone should be, we "dis-member" them from the divine. When we create sacred space for healing, we open the space for others to heal. Each of us can be healers, but only for ourselves. Each of us can create the space for healing for others to find healing within themselves.

Letting Go of Judgment

WE DO NOT NEED TO ALL AGREE ON ONE PATH. To heal ourselves, others and the world around us, we need every path to the divine, not just one. The path to the divine that I choose for myself, if forced upon someone else, does not lead them to the divine. We each have within us the knowledge of what will lead us to the divine and, when the conditions are right, we find that path. If a path manifests love in the world, it contains Truth and leads us to the divine. If it does not manifest love in the world, it misses the mark and we have the responsibility to realign ourselves with the divine. A path that generates stigma, judgment and isolation is not a path to the divine.

Stigma is Collective Fear

STIGMA IS THE ROOT OF ALL ILLNESS in our world. Stigma is a fear of difference, driven by judgment, resulting in ignorance and isolation. The greatest wounding experiences in our collective human history have all been generated and perpetuated by stigma. Stigma of Africans led to slavery. Stigma of native peoples led to the conquest of the Americas. Stigma of Jews and Gypsies led to the Holocaust. Stigma of the Hutus and Tutsis led to the genocide

Chapter 5

in Rwanda. Stigma of HIV/AIDS is perpetuating the pandemic around the world today. These are a few examples among many of how humans have lived down to their woundedness instead of living up to their divine essence. Stigma is a collective judgment that a category of people is less than divine.

Stigma creates ignorance and isolation for both the person stigmatizing and the person being stigmatized. Stigma creates disease in the physical body, mental illness in the cognitive/emotional bodies, and separation in the spiritual body. Compassion, the antidote for stigma, creates knowledge and connection for both the person being compassionate and the person receiving compassion. Compassion creates health in the physical, cognitive/emotional, and spiritual bodies by reconnecting us to each other and to the divine. Compassion heals, makes us hale, brings us to wholeness.

> *He who thinks alone grows peculiar.*
>
> *- Unknown*

Each of us, in every moment, has the opportunity to choose between stigma and compassion. Each of us, in every moment, has the opportunity to see others as divine. When we see others as divine, they begin to become more divine. They begin to become what we see in them. If we see their limitations and shortcomings, they grow down to those. If we see their potential and divinity, they grow up to those. The exact same process a divine warrior employs to grow into her or his own divine potential is employed to recognize the divine in others.

Minimum Conditions for Human Existence

WE ALL HAVE BASIC HUMAN SURVIVAL NEEDS which must be met before we can attend to our healing. When basic human survival needs are not met, we continue to be wounded and live out of that woundedness because all of our energies are focused on survival. Safe water, healthy food, adequate clothing and shelter, and a safe place to sleep and recharge are all minimum conditions for human existence. Until these needs are met, we cannot expect healing to occur. The systems we have created in this world are not adequately addressing these most basic human needs for the majority of the humans on the planet. As we begin to heal ourselves and create the space for those around us to heal, transforming our systems to provide basic human needs for all is essential. Once our basic human needs are met, healing of wounds can occur at a

Chapter 5

greater and greater pace.

The Greatest Gift

THE GREATEST GIFT ONE HUMAN CAN OFFER to another is safe space to heal and grow. In fact, all other gifts pale in comparison to the value of pure, gentle, warm and healing space for the wounds of the world to heal – for the natural process of becoming hale and whole again.

This healing space holds such value because it is vital to full living, it is the natural condition of life, and it reconnects us to each other and to the divine. Space for healing is vital to living in that it allows us to recover and regain our strength to go on. We all know people who feel so battered by the events in their lives that they have lost hope. These dear souls go through life with little zest, going through the motions, often letting off the pressure of their torture by pushing it off onto those around them. They have lost their vitality for life, lost the joy of simply being alive. I believe that this condition is created and perpetuated by a lack of safe space for healing.

Safe space for healing is the natural condition of life. Life is not meant to be a relentless struggle from start to finish, no matter how we have manifested in the material plane. For example, plants have their seasons of growth, stretching, and expanding, as well as their seasons of rest, turning within, and sending down roots to stand taller and stronger in the gusts of life. Animals find safe places away from their predators where they can rest and gain strength for the tasks of finding food and companionship. Humans have these needs too. In spite of these needs, humans are the genesis of most, if not all, of the trauma we experience. Perhaps this is why many end up walking around wounded instead of seeking a safe place for healing – the places we have chosen in the past have not turned out to be as safe as we thought or hoped. A seemingly natural condition of life is twisted into something less.

When we create safe space for healing, it reconnects us to each other. Setting our intention to love another in this way opens our heart to accept and receive them in their unique journey. None of us shares exactly the same path, that mix of what we bring into the world and what the world brings to us. What is a wound for one goes unnoticed by another. Each wound brings with it the opportunity to transform it, but to do so, we need safe space. I may be able to create safe space for myself and heal some of my

Chapter 5

wounds. Nevertheless, I am left with other wounds that cannot be healed on my own. These remaining wounds are somehow "relational:" they arise out of, or need the healing conditions of, not just myself, but myself in relation to another. For these wounds, safe space for healing is the greatest gift we can give each other, for it reestablishes a healthy connection, a healthy relation to others. In this way it reconnects us to the divine as well, recreating the bond between matter and spirit. I believe there is one essential condition for creating safe space for healing that generates all these benefits.

This one essential condition for creating safe space is love. When I say love, I am not talking about a human emotion or the commercialized misappropriation of the word that equates it to buying something for someone. I am talking about the energetic life force spoken of by all the master teachers of the world. Sharing this energetic life force with another is simple, and often not easy. It requires attention to the entire encounter with another: our coming together, our time together and our moving apart. All three of these facets of being together hold the risk of love being reduced into something less. At any moment the safe space can shift into space with an agenda.

Our coming together holds the risk of judgment – attributing the wounds of another to some lack within them, to their unworthiness. This risk bears itself out in many ways. For example, questioning why someone was in the place they were in when they were wounded, thereby placing blame on the wounded for the wound they received. Love means nonjudgment in our coming together: knowing that we know little about another's path; knowing their path has been perfect for them; and knowing their path has brought them to an opportunity to heal.

Our time together holds the risk of imposing our agenda on the wounded. Many of us have experienced situations where the space has been represented as safe and sacred, we have taken the representations on trust, and once in the space come to the realization that there is an agenda not fully revealed to us prior to our trust. We can feel violated when this happens because what we receive is something less than love. Love means respect for the process of another without imposing our agenda on the unfolding of another's path and process. It means watching a flower bloom instead of bruising it by pushing the petals apart. Love means sharing safe space with another and sitting in awe and reverence in their presence.

Our moving apart holds the risk of using another to satisfy our own needs. There are many places in the world where one can seek help, and help will only continue to flow if there is some outward indication of progress. Love means holding safe space for healing and being unattached to the outcome. Healing is not always dramatic. Healing is not always able to be put into language. Healing is not always noticeable in the moment. Healing is most easily done in safe space we can create for each other. Safe space for healing is the greatest gift of love.

> *The success of love is in the loving*
> *- it is not in the result of loving.*
> *Of course it is natural in love*
> *to want the best for the other person,*
> *but whether it turns out that way*
> *or not does not determine the value*
> *of what we have done.*
>
> *- Mother Teresa*

COMPASSION IN OUR DAILY LIVES

A DIVINE WARRIOR'S RELATIONSHIP WITH OTHER requires a commitment to living compassion. We all know compassion when we see it. It is in a person stepping out of the way so someone less mobile can get on the bus first. It is a "Good Morning" or "Hello" to a person at the counter. It is eye contact and a smile with no other agenda than to brighten someone's day. It is holding the door open for the person following behind you. It is sharing a load up or down the stairs for a person with a stroller, a suitcase, or a shopping cart. We see these acts of compassion every day in our lives and the world is a better place because of them. Divine warriors recognize the power of these acts and practice them, thereby manifesting the divine in the material plane.

> *Sorrow shared is halved, joy shared is doubled.*
>
> *- William Blake*

As long as one of us remains wounded, we are all wounded.

A slogan for healing others:

Choose Compassion

CHAPTER 5

ADDITIONAL RESOURCES FOR CHAPTER 5

1.   Baldwin, Christina. (1998). *Calling the Circle: The First and Future Culture*. New York, Bantam Books. ISBN # 978-0-553-37900-6 www.bantam.com

> Ms. Baldwin and her organization, PeerSpirit have brought working in circle back into our consciousness and culture. A wonderful way for creating sacred space together as equals.

2.   Ilibagiza, Immaculée (2007). *Left to Tell: Discovering God Amidst the Rwandan Holocaust*. Carlsbad, CA: Hay House. ISBN # 1-4019-0897-7   www.hayhouse.com

> This book is one of the most inspiring stories of horror, forgiveness and compassion that I have ever read. It sets new heights to our potential as humans to survive and forgive.

3.   Palmer, Parker J. (2004). *A Hidden Wholeness: The Journey toward an Undivided Life*. San Francisco: Jossey-Bass. ISBN # 978-0-7879-7100-6   www.josseybass.com

> A guide through the process of creating circles of trust where our souls can emerge and speak their truth in response to the challenges we are facing in our lives.

4.   Wheatley, Margaret (2002). *Turning to One Another: Simple Conversations to Restore Hope to the Future*. San Francisco: Berrett-

Koehler Publishers. ISBN # 978-1-576751459

www.bkconnection.com

> Provides several conversation starters on topics that are vital to building community and trust.

CHAPTER 6

HEALING OUR WORLD

DIVINE WARRIORS ARE ON THE PATH to heal themselves and create the space for others to heal. As human healing proceeds, we come to realize that the ripples of healing must extend beyond human, to all that is. We must evolve our consciousness to recognize the divine in everything. When we see everything as divine, we engage it with respect and love.

Healing our world requires nothing less than complete surrender – surrendering every shred of consciousness of our lives as limited, separated individuals to an expanded consciousness of our lives as an unlimited, connected collective. To heal our world, we must see it as an inseparable part of us, not some object to manage, but an essential aspect of who we are. We do not need to "save the planet," we need to save ourselves from the consciousness that has put the livability of our planet in peril. When we surrender our lives to the divine as divine warriors, we come to realize our purpose in this world is service.

> *From Wanka Tanka, the Great Spirit, there came a great unifying life force that flowed in and through all things - the flowers of the plains, blowing winds, rocks, trees, birds, animals - and was the same force that had been breathed into the first man. Thus all things were kindred and were brought together by the same Great Mystery.*
>
> *- Chief Luther Standing Bear Oglala Sioux (1868-1939)*

Divine Warriors as Stewards

AS WE GROW TO SEE EVERYTHING AS DIVINE, we move into a consciousness of stewardship. Stewardship recognizes the divine nature of that which we are in relationship. It recognizes the aspects of the divine that come into our field of influence as gifts to be used only as needed and otherwise maintained for the good of all. We cannot own the divine. We can steward the divine. Ownership has taken us too far down the path of rights. Stewardship takes us down the path of responsibility. When all of the divine that has manifested is ours to steward, we have no need to waste, no need to use up, no need to hoard. Our individual right to use as stewards is no greater than the rights of other parts of the divine to use. As stewards, our right to cut down a tree is weighed against not only the rights of others to have the tree produce oxygen, but also the rights of other creatures to use the tree for their life.

If we take a wider view, say one that looks at life from a 1000-year snapshot, we can clearly see that none of us owns anything: not cars, not houses, not land, not even our bodies. We are all short-term tenants, occupying a small amount of space for a brief amount of time. As tenants, our landlord is the divine. How are we treating the landlord's property? Are we being good stewards, limiting our use, minimizing our damage, living in the knowledge that those who follow us will need the same basic conditions for human existence? As stewards we are gardeners of this planet. Are we creating a beautiful garden that sustains itself? Are we creating a garden that will be habitable in 1000 years? It is our responsibility as stewards to do so.

Stewards recognize that they are part of something bigger, that they have responsibility to something greater than their own needs

> *For unto whom much is given, of him shall much be required.*
>
> *- Luke 12:48 (KJV)*

and desires. A steward's own needs are part of the equation, but not the entire equation. A steward attends to her or his needs in order to be able to be an effective steward. Stewards serve the greater good rather than focusing on their personal needs.

Becoming a Steward

BECOMING A STEWARD REQUIRES a consciousness that expands into an awareness of abundance and trust. Abundance is all around us; it is our legacy and is available in all places at all times. Abundance is there whether we see it or not. It is not about material possessions as much as it is about a state of mind. Abundance is to optimism as scarcity is to pessimism. It is seeing the water that is present in the glass and not comparing it to the rim to see whether it is half full or half empty. With an abundance consciousness, the water is enough for our current needs. Abundance consciousness reminds us that, in this moment, we have everything we need. It helps us to live in the moment, letting go of the past, realizing there is no future other than now. In the midst of living in the moment, we train ourselves to focus on what we have been provided, not what might have been or what would feel good to have someday. Today. Now. In this moment I have enough. There is nothing I need in this moment to live and love. When we expand into this consciousness, we know abundance permeates our experience.

The second element of becoming a steward and expanding into an abundance consciousness is interwoven with the first: trust. To live in an abundance consciousness one must release any concerns for the future into the divine, cultivating a deep and abiding sense of trust that we are cared for no matter what may come. This sense of trust comes to us easiest when our consciousness is expanded to a place where we see our life as but an instant of time in our greater existence. When we recognize that we are divine, our material experience becomes insignificant, shorter than a blink of the eye. Putting our lives into this perspective helps us to see that we are all-ways and all-times nurtured and loved. The divine surrounds us, envelops us, and permeates us. Being connected to everything, we have everything available to us.

Trust is a choice we make. When we begin to make the choice to trust, it can be scary and overwhelming. We can begin with small things, looking at whether they worked out for us over time, not whether we received exactly what we wanted when we wanted it. As we begin to trust, we begin to surrender more and more of our life to the divine, knowing that there is a larger plan at play than we can see in our limited perception. Life does not necessarily become easier or more comfortable, but it does become more meaningful as we look past the thread of disappointment or pain and see it woven into the beautiful tapestry of our path through the world. When we choose trust, unexpected events become exciting opportunities containing the potential of new openings and joy. When we choose trust, working towards one's purpose becomes a path shared with the divine instead of a seemingly solitary venture. As we attune ourselves to hearing, seeing, feeling and knowing the divine is with us, we become aware of all the openings along our path that provide assistance on the way: like looking past the thorns that might tear our skin to see the flowers that brighten our day.

Trust is much deeper than hope. Trust is a knowing that no

matter what happens, our divine essence cannot be extinguished or altered in any way or under any circumstance. Trust is looking for the message in the events of our life. For example, if we get locked out of the house or out of our vehicle, what is the deeper meaning for our life in that event? In what way is the event a message from the divine? If we find ourselves locked out of our house, are we somehow "locking ourselves out" of nurturing, safe space in our life? If we find ourselves locked out of our vehicle, are we somehow "locking ourselves out" of our mobility, out of moving around? If we cannot find meaning in the event as a message about our life, then perhaps it is an event connected to a bigger series of events that have not yet manifested. Perhaps we missed an airplane flight that then provided us the opportunity to meet someone on the next flight that can assist us on our path and vice versa. If we get caught up in the disappointment and frustration of missing the flight, we may also miss the opportunity.

Living as Steward

AS MY TRUST IN THE DIVINE GROWS DEEPER, I find that I grow to trust and love my divine essence more. I am gentler and more forgiving of my thoughts, actions and speech that fall short of the legacy of my divine essence. In addition to the gentler and more forgiving approach to myself, I am gentler and more forgiving of the thoughts, actions and speech of others that fall short of the legacy of their divine essence. Living in this trust is a place of calm and peace. As we "re-member" ourselves and others to the divine, judgment falls away. What remains is gratitude. And, what arises out of this profound sense of gratitude is service. Not service that expects recognition or reward in return, but service as a spontaneous song of singularity. When I am divine and you are divine and all that which has been created is divine, service becomes simply joining the joyous chorus of celebration. When service arises out of gratitude, we lose all sense of "you" and "other," and we become one. Hindus have a Sanskrit word for this experience, "Namaste."

Ascent to the Mountain Top

Because we are in the material plane, we cannot completely lose ourselves in this chorus. We must continue to care for and heal ourselves as we join this chorus. Another analogy might help to understand the balance to strike between caring for ourselves and caring for the world. We can say that "re-membering" ourselves to the divine is the top of a mountain. Divine warriors have set

CHAPTER 6

their goal of reaching the mountain peak. There are innumerable paths to the peak and each of us must find our own unique way, which may include the path of others for a time, but in the end only we know what is right for us. As we prepare for our ascent to the peak, we know that there are two essential elements for a successful ascent. First, we must have a nurturing, supportive base camp. At base camp we rest, refuel, and wait out severe weather. We also plan our path and gather the wisdom of others to make our ascent easier. Without a good base camp, we would perish in our attempt to reach the peak. However good a base camp is, it is still not enough.

The second essential element for a successful ascent to the peak is to leave base camp and set out toward the peak. No amount of resting, refueling, planning or gathering the wisdom of others will get us to the peak without actually putting one foot in front of the other in the world. The peak of the mountain cannot be reached without actually traveling our path. To successfully manifest the divine in this world, we must both gather our strength in base camp and use that strength to make the ascent to the peak. Some of us have become comfortable in base camp, spending our lives gathering our strength. Some of us are out making our ascent ignoring the need for a base camp, spending our lives pushing on at the edge of our stamina. We do our most effective work when we balance time in base camp with striking out for the peak.

Each of us must find our own path to the peak. Each path is the right path for that climber. Every path is needed. All paths can be service. One path might be through the business sector, perhaps as a divine warrior accountant. One path might be through the health sector, as a divine warrior nurse; or as a divine warrior janitor, or truck driver, or developer, or attorney, or mother, or foster parent, or writer, or electrician, or convenience store clerk. In every moment and every setting we are provided an opportunity to think, act and speak out of the divine. Becoming a divine warrior does not require changing the situation, it requires changing our consciousness and bringing that consciousness into everything we are and every situation in which we find ourselves. It requires recognizing that we are divine. It requires recognizing that other humans are divine. It requires recognizing that all creation is divine. And once this recognition takes hold, we move into the final phase of the evolution of human consciousness, returning to

Chapter 6

divine consciousness simultaneously with being in human form. We surrender to service. We become divine warriors.

> *A slogan for healing the world:*
> # Surrender to Service

CHAPTER 7

A Few Words for the Christians among Us

EVERYTHING WRITTEN IN THIS BOOK is consistent with the teachings of our brother Jesus. The extent to which what has been said does not resonate with your understanding of the New Testament is the extent to which we have drifted in the last 2000 years from the essence of Jesus' message. The New Testament contains both words attributed to Jesus as well as commentary on Jesus' purpose, skills and challenges. Jesus was truly a divine warrior. This book does not have the space to provide an exhaustive statement of Jesus as divine warrior, and it is important to illustrate the parallels of Jesus' message to the contents of this book. With a mind open to the expansiveness and radical nature of Jesus' message, we can see the consistencies. With a mind closed to anything more than a predetermined set of rules handed down over time by authority figures, we will see only an attack on the tradition we have learned. Jesus did not teach tradition. Jesus taught to transcend tradition, living into the core values of love of self, other and the divine.

Relationship with Self

IN LUKE 17, VERSES 20 AND 21, Jesus is reported to have said:

> [20] And when he was demanded of the Pharisees, when the kingdom of God should come, he answered them and said, The kingdom of God cometh not with observation:
> [21] Neither shall they say, Lo here! or, lo there! for, behold, the kingdom of God is within you. (KJV)

Jesus told the Pharisees that the kingdom of God is within them. The Pharisees were not Jesus' followers, family or friends. They were people opposed to his message and still he reminded them that they have divine essence within them. His message is loud and clear: we all are of divine essence. Early commentators of Jesus' life and words also understood this radical message. The writer of

Chapter 7

Acts, in chapter 17, reports of Paul's visit to Athens:

> [22] Then Paul stood in the midst of Mars' hill, and said, Ye men of Athens, I perceive that in all things ye are too superstitious.
>
> [23] For as I passed by, and beheld your devotions, I found an altar with this inscription, TO THE UNKNOWN GOD. Whom therefore ye ignorantly worship, him declare I unto you.
>
> [24] God that made the world and all things therein, seeing that he is Lord of heaven and earth, dwelleth not in temples made with hands;
>
> [25] Neither is worshipped with men's hands, as though he needed any thing, seeing he giveth to all life, and breath, and all things;
>
> [26] And hath made of one blood all nations of men for to dwell on all the face of the earth, and hath determined the times before appointed, and the bounds of their habitation;
>
> [27] That they should seek the Lord, if haply they might feel after him, and find him, though he be not far from every one of us:
>
> [28] For in him we live, and move, and have our being; as certain also of your own poets have said, For we are also his offspring. (KJV)

If we live, and move, and have our being in the divine, how can we not be of divine essence? Are we like rocks of non-divine around which runs water of divine? We are clearly divine and can only be separated from it in our illusions of separateness. In verse 28, Paul calls us God's offspring, and repeats it again in verse 29. In all of creation, what does a particular kind of life give birth to, but offspring of the same? The offspring of a rose is not a roach. The offspring of a dog is not a dandelion. The offspring of God is not a godless human. A rose gives birth to a rose. A dog gives birth to a dog. The divine gives birth to the divine.

The writer of the second letter to the Corinthians was clear about the process of living into our divine legacy when he said in chapter 3:

> [16] Nevertheless when it shall turn to the Lord, the veil shall be taken away.
> [17] Now the Lord is that Spirit: and where the Spirit of the Lord is, there is liberty.
> [18] But we all, with open face beholding as in a glass [mirror] the glory of the Lord, are changed into the same image from glory to glory, even as by the Spirit of the Lord. (KJV)

Being transformed from glory into glory in the same image of the divine is absolutely the same process described in this book. It is our collective purpose as humans: to manifest the divine in this material plane. Being a divine warrior is stepping into the legacy referenced in the New Testament.

Relationship with Other

CENTRAL TO THE LIFE AND WORDS OF JESUS is a radical approach to how we treat our fellow humans. Christianity has certainly advanced our understanding (and to some extent our practice) of how to treat others. Most current Christian traditions have gone astray from Jesus' message by placing Jesus in a separate category of human, something his life and words never did. The following passage attributed to Jesus from Matthew 25 illustrates Jesus' core teaching on relationship with other:

> [31] When the Son of man shall come in his glory, and all the holy angels with him, then shall he sit upon the throne of his glory:
> [32] And before him shall be gathered all nations: and he shall separate them one from another, as a shepherd divideth his sheep from the goats:
> [33] And he shall set the sheep on his right hand, but the goats on the left.
> [34] Then shall the King say unto them on his right hand, Come, ye blessed of my Father, inherit the kingdom prepared for you from the foundation of the world:

> ³⁵ For I was an hungred, and ye gave me meat: I was thirsty, and ye gave me drink: I was a stranger, and ye took me in:
> ³⁶ Naked, and ye clothed me: I was sick, and ye visited me: I was in prison, and ye came unto me.
> ³⁷ Then shall the righteous answer him, saying, Lord, when saw we thee an hungred, and fed thee? or thirsty, and gave thee drink?
> ³⁸ When saw we thee a stranger, and took thee in? or naked, and clothed thee?
> ³⁹ Or when saw we thee sick, or in prison, and came unto thee?
> ⁴⁰ And the King shall answer and say unto them, Verily I say unto you, Inasmuch as ye have done it unto one of the least of these my brethren, ye have done it unto me. (KJV)

Most of us familiar with the New Testament know that this passage goes on in verse 46 to send some into eternal punishment and others into life eternal. To show kindness to our fellow humans based on the prospect of eternal punishment is to act out of fear, with values imposed externally. To show kindness to our fellow humans based on the consciousness that they contain divine essence is to practice the core value of living-kindness. Jesus said that the people we meet in this world who are in need are interchangeable with him. The way we treat others is the way we treat the divine. Jesus' radical message was not that he is the son of God, but that we all are sons and daughters of the divine.

Relationship with Divine

JESUS WAS A BEAUTIFUL MODEL of being in constant relationship with the divine. His life was a prayer. One of the most recognized passages attributed to Jesus is what we have come to call "the Lord's Prayer." For many Christians, this beloved passage has become a mantra, recited word for word with exactly the same phrasing and pace each time it is spoken. In the West, the Christian traditions rely on early versions of the books of the New Testament written in Koine Greek, one of the common languages spoken in the time and place Jesus lived. Greek was the language of the ruling political system of the time. Most biblical scholars agree Jesus probably spoke Greek. In the Eastern Christian traditions, the early versions of the books of the New Testament were written in Aramaic, the local common language in the time and place Jesus lived. Most biblical scholars agree Jesus' native language was Aramaic. The Aramaic language holds within its phrases layers of meaning, providing the listener to develop a relationship with the depth of the phrasing. Greek is much more exacting, less lyrical. While Aramaic is symbolic,

Greek is literal. Neither Greek nor Aramaic versions of the books of the New Testament hold the exclusive access to the truth of Jesus' words; both can provide us access to the essence of Jesus' relationship with the divine. As we see the two translations side by side, perhaps we will see more clearly how Jesus practiced living-surrender in his relationship with divine:

The Lord's Prayer (Matthew 6:9-13, (KJV)	**The Lord's Prayer** (One possible new translation from the Aramaic)
⁹ After this manner therefore pray ye:	
Our Father which art in heaven,	O Birther! Father-Mother of the Cosmos,
Hallowed be thy name.	Focus your light within us – make it useful:
¹⁰ Thy kingdom come,	Create your reign of unity now
Thy will be done in earth, as it is in heaven.	Your one desire then acts with ours, as in all light, so in all forms.
¹¹ Give us this day our daily bread.	Grant what we need each day in bread and insight.

Chapter 7

[12] And forgive us our debts, as we forgive our debtors.	Loose the cords of mistakes binding us, as we release the strands we hold of others' guilt.
[13] And lead us not into temptation, but deliver us from evil:	Don't let surface things delude us, but free us from what holds us back.
For thine is the kingdom, and the power, and the glory, for ever.	From you is born all ruling will, the power and the life to do, the song that beautifies all, from age to age it renews.
Amen.	Truly – power to these statements – may be the ground from which all my actions grow: Amen.

Douglas-Klotz, N. (1990). Prayers of the Cosmos: Meditations on the Aramaic Words of Jesus, p. 41. New York: HarperSanFrancisco.

The trinity of relationships, relationship with self, other and divine, is found in a single verse in the Old Testament, Micah 6:8, which states: "He hath shewed thee, O man, what is good; and what doth the Lord require of thee, but to do justly, and to love mercy, and to walk humbly with thy God?"

The Messiah Agenda

THE TEACHINGS AND DOCTRINE of the books comprising the New Testament are varied and diverse. There are places of inconsistency between books as well as within books. Each book was selected by men to be included in the New Testament, and there surely was heated and fierce discussion of what to include and what to exclude. What helps each of the books chosen to hang together in a unified whole is what could be called the "messiah agenda." The messiah agenda continues today. It is an intentional and concerted effort on the part of a select group of men to set up Jesus as God, to promote Jesus as the only path to God, and to set up this select group of men to be the only intermediaries between Jesus as God and the peoples of the earth. If, as untold millions have come to believe over the last 20 centuries, Jesus is the Messiah, the savior of mankind, then he exerts incredible power over our

Chapter 7

lives. If Jesus taught we each must transform our lives to come into alignment and relationship with the divine, Jesus was a beautiful example of that transformational process and he is our fellow traveler, our brother in the process. The difference between Jesus as the only path to the divine and Jesus as fellow traveler on the path to the divine is the messiah agenda. The messiah agenda has been advanced through the entire spectrum of influence known to man: benevolence, love, parenting, culture, reason, persuasion, ecstatic experience, coercion, maiming, rape, torture, death, genocide, and all other means of humans exerting power over other humans.

Let us imagine, if we can, that we were not born into the 4000+ years of JudeoChristian tradition that we have been immersed in all our life. Imagine also, if we can, that our view of history is not bound by the perspective of someone who lives less than 100 years and was born toward the end of the second century. So if we do not have the limitations of perspective of having been raised in a culture where Christianity is the dominant religion and we have the ability to see across the expanse of 2000 years of human history in which Christianity originated, grew and flourished, what would we see? Undoubtedly, we would see acts of unselfish love performed by individuals in the name of Jesus. And yes, we would see various attempts, with varying success, by groups of people calling themselves Christians, to address poverty, injustice and oppression.

In addition to these acts inspired by the example of Jesus, we would see, in our 2000 year view, a sustained, systematic, and often brutal effort by a few to use Christianity to exercise power over others. Those who use the life and words of Jesus to exercise power over others will be most disturbed by this book because they have the most to lose by a change in the world's current cosmology. Those who use the life and words of Jesus to exercise power over others have changed Jesus' message of revolution and love into a message of domination and power over. They may feel their domination and power threatened and may seek to discredit or discount the call to live into our legacy from the divine. Our task, no matter the calls to the contrary, is to manifest the divine in all circumstances.

Living out our Common Legacy with Jesus

BY NOW, YOU MAY HAVE COME TO AN UNDERSTANDING that most of what is said in this book may be viewed as "heresy" by

Chapter 7

Christians promoting the messiah agenda. The very word heresy comes from a Greek word meaning choice. Heresy means to choose to believe something different from the official beliefs. Based on this definition, Jesus was the ultimate heretic, a Jew who rejected the official beliefs of the day, choosing to live into the divine legacy we all share. You have the head and the heart to discern whether the material in this book rings true to you, and you have a choice of whether to continue to hold on to creed and tradition or find your own path and relationship with the divine. Should you find yourself at the crossroads, this chapter is offered as an introduction into a more expansive awareness of Jesus' life and words.

Jesus did not come into this world to establish a new religion. Jesus came into this world to announce a new consciousness - a new consciousness that transcended the consciousness of the world in which he walked. A new consciousness of our legacy from Yahweh, the great I Am. This new consciousness is one that requires our participation in the mind of God. It requires our awakened participation in the world in which we find ourselves. Jesus did not seek to create a new human institution we now call Christianity, he came to invite us into a more expansive awareness of the divine. His call was not to modify the world as we found it, but to engage the world in a completely different way. He did not usher in a transition, but a transformation.

Christians are trained to wait for the second coming, but the second coming is here and now. It is in every moment. It is in each choice we make. It is in each breath. It is in each birth of a new life with all its potential. The second coming is in each time we choose to live into our sacred relationships with self, other and divine. In this way, we invite Christ to come right now, in this moment. Jesus did not die for your sins, Jesus died for his values. Jesus died for the values of living-authentic, living-kindness, and living-surrender. Jesus was a divine warrior. His life and words invited us to become divine warriors also.

Additional Resources for Chapter 7:

Douglas-Klotz, Neil (2006). *Blessings of the Cosmos: Wisdom of the Heart from the Aramaic Words of Jesus*. Boulder, CO: Sounds True. ISBN # 1-59179-417-X www.soundstrue.com

Section II: Divine Warrior Training Exercises

Intention

DIVINE WARRIOR EXERCISES ARE AN IMPORTANT PART of Divine Warrior Training. All skills improve with practice, even if you have a natural affinity toward that skill. These exercises are primarily intended to expand your view of the world, and some of them, where noted, have a particular focus. None of them is cast in stone. They are all effective when you engage with them and stretch yourself to see your world in a new way. So, I invite you to modify them as you need to in order to make them applicable to your life, and refrain from the urge to make them so easy that they do not "call you out" into a more expansive view of the world.

Reading them with your rational mind will not give you the full effect of each exercise. Trying to do so would be like looking at a poster of a movie and saying that you do not need to see the movie because you understood the poster. Or like saying that seeing the mouth of the cave is enough to know what the entire cave holds. While some of these exercises may seem simplistic on their surface, they will all hold deep openings for you if you engage them with your heart in a space where you can safely take your time.

Setting

I HAVE COME TO KNOW THAT EACH OF US contains divine essence. This essence is "sufficient unto all things," needing only the proper conditions to sprout, grow, flower and regenerate with seeds of like kind. The conditions necessary for the unfolding of our divine essence are simple: 1) basic needs of water, food, shelter and clothing, and 2) a safe and sacred space. It is still possible for the unfolding of divine essence to occur without these conditions, but it is a more difficult process.

These exercises can be done on your own or in a group of two or more. You may want to start on your own, and as you

Section II

expand into your divine essence, the next step may be finding or creating a Divine Warrior Training Group. As discussed earlier in this book, creating sacred space together is an important part of healing our world and I would highly recommend it. We all need companions along our path.

When you are ready to engage in an exercise, start by creating a safe and sacred space. It is important that the space you create be free of distractions and interruptions for a minimum of one hour – a two hour space is ideal so you will not feel rushed. Select some calming, soothing music to play and have a journal or some writing paper ready. If you have any interest in art or crafts (notice I did not say talent), have those supplies ready as well.

Find a meditation practice that helps you get quiet and calm. Focusing on your breath is a simple technique that is used in many spiritual traditions. Here is an abbreviated version of one I use often in Divine Warrior Training Circles:

> Find a comfortable place to sit, getting comfortable in your body. Give yourself permission to spend some time loving and caring for yourself. On your next inhalation, follow your breath into your lungs, imagining you can follow the

life-giving oxygen carried by your blood to all cells in your body. As the blood releases the life-giving oxygen, imagine you can follow the blood back to your heart and then to your lungs, completing the cycle. Repeat with as many breaths as you need to feel quiet and calm, present in the moment. Once you are quiet and calm, find your Sacred Heart, a space behind your physical heart, where you can stand before a door into your inner wisdom, the wisdom of the divine. Stand before the door until you are ready to step into your wisdom. Then open the door and step through.

After you have accessed your inner wisdom, select an exercise to work on and spend time with it, staying in your heart center. One way of accessing divine guidance is to allow spirit to select an exercise for you. This can be done easily by holding the book closed in your hands and letting it fall open to an exercise. That exercise, whatever it is, is the one spirit has led you to for this time. Doing some artwork or craft work can serve to distract your mind so you can hear the wisdom of your heart.

At first you may find it difficult to make the time in your life to engage in the Divine Warrior Training exercise process. If this is the case, one way to proceed is to create a Divine Warrior Training

Group that meets regularly, for example once or twice a month, to support each other. This group can create and hold the space for each participant as they engage the Divine Warrior Training exercises. You can select a leader who will guide the meditation, or take turns. Creating this group using the ancient tradition of circle (see books by Baldwin and Palmer listed at the end of this section) helps each participant find the space to do her or his own work while holding sacred space for each of the others in the group.

Additional Resources for Section II:

1. Baldwin, Christina (1998). *Calling the Circle: The First and Future Culture.* New York, Bantam Books. ISBN # 978-0553379006, www.randomhouse.com

2. Palmer, Parker J. (2004). *A Hidden Wholeness: The Journey Toward an Undivided Life.* San Francisco, Jossey-Bass. ISBN # 978-0787971007, www.jossey-bass.com

Divine Warrior Training

Exercise 1: Your Personal Cosmology

We live in a culture where we are trained to focus primarily on our individual lives. If represented in a diagram, with your life represented as the space between the parentheses, this view looks like this:

??(--)??

What if our individual lives were viewed from a different perspective, say in relation to eternity, or the age of the universe, or the age of the earth, or even the age of mankind? If represented in a diagram, with your life represented as the space between the parentheses, this view looks like this:

--()--

Please answer the following three questions to the best of your ability

1. Which diagram or cosmology would you say most closely represents your view of your life?
2. What are your hopes/beliefs/understandings of who, where or what you were before you were born into this material existence? Also, describe the certainty you have of your view and what experiences you have had supporting this view.
3. What are your hopes/beliefs/understandings of who, where or what you will be after your life ends? Also, describe the certainty you have of your view and what experiences you have had to come to this view.

SECTION II

NOTES FROM THE SACRED HEART:

Divine Warrior Training

Exercise 2: Viewing Your Life from the Moon

Imagine you are standing on the moon. If you were standing on the moon, the earth would appear in the sky about the size of a quarter laying on this paper.

1. How significant is your life on earth when viewed from the moon?

2. How significant are the problems in your life when viewed from the perspective of the moon?

SECTION II

NOTES FROM THE SACRED HEART:

Divine Warrior Training

Exercise 3: My Life Review

Write a short non-fiction essay about your life – somewhere in between an obituary and an autobiography. Include in it all the major accomplishments and disappointments. If you would like, also write about what will happen in the future in your life: what is yet to come for you and how do you see yourself dying?

SECTION II

NOTES FROM THE SACRED HEART:

Exercise 4: Contact with the Other Side

Who do you know in your life that has died? Choose one person you were close to and then take a few minutes to be silent. Once you have found a still place, imagine he or she has come to you to describe what happens when one dies. Listen carefully and take notes if you care to.

SECTION II

NOTES FROM THE SACRED HEART:

Divine Warrior Training

Exercise 5: "To Die For"

For what cause or person would you be willing to die? Describe the qualities of that person or cause that brings you to that willingness. Are there other causes or people for whom you would die? What do they have in common? What are their differences?

SECTION II

NOTES FROM THE SACRED HEART:

Exercise 6: Self Forgiveness

We are all wounded and we have all wounded others. Over time, there are choices we have made in the past that we come to regret or wish we could have made a different choice. Often, we hold on to those ideas of our past well beyond the time that they are useful to our lives. These ideas of the past are like cables, ropes or threads pulling us back into the past and draining our energy.

Choose today one thing that you are ready to be done with - one choice from your past that did not work out well that you would like to let go of. Perhaps you stayed in a job too long, or in a marriage too long, and once you got out you beat yourself up for taking so long. Perhaps you turned down an opportunity that later appeared to be an excellent choice. Perhaps you started a relationship that looked good from the outset, but turned out poorly, dragging you down into actions and words that you are ashamed of.

Now that you have chosen something from your past you are ready to be done with, follow the seven steps outlined below to achieve self forgiveness.

1. RECOGNIZE   [You recognize that a being was harmed (this could be yourself who was harmed) from your action or inaction.]

2. REMORSE   [You feel bad for the harm that was done and your part in it.]

3. "RE-ACT"   [You change your behavior so that the harm will not happen again.]

4. REPAIR   [If possible or practicable, you seek to "make it right."

Section II

Some possibilities of REPAIR might include asking forgiveness, making restitution, or working toward reconciliation.]

5. RECONCILE [You recognize that the choice you made has provided you with knowledge that you did not have at the time you originally made the choice.]

6. RELEASE [You release yourself from an impossible standard: you are judging yourself for past choices based on current understanding. Instead, choose to believe the following statement: "I did the best I could at the time I made the choice given the information I had at the time."]

7. RITUAL [This step is limited only by your creativity. Use your intuition to decide what is appropriate. Perhaps you could write a letter to yourself (or someone else) and then burn it or tear it up. Perhaps there are objects in your home that represent the choice you are releasing yourself from and you are ready to let them go. Perhaps you want to light a candle. Perhaps you want to "cut" the cable, rope or thread that has been draining your energy to this past event. Some ritual, however simple, will help you be done and seal the release.]

Notes from the Sacred Heart:

Exercise 7: Parts of the Whole

Imagine that the dominant perception in western society of individual lives and relationships is not true. Imagine further that the truth is that each "person," including you, is a single cell of a larger organism: all of humanity is one large organism which is unaware of itself as a separate entity. Stated differently, you and every one you meet are cells in a larger structure. Were this true, would this change the way you relate to others? If so, how?

SECTION II

NOTES FROM THE SACRED HEART:

Exercise 8: Job

The book of Job in the Old Testament is a narrative of a divine experiment between the universe (or God) and the power of evil in the material world. The experiment tests the effects of the power of evil on human consciousness or, more specifically, a man's belief in God. Imagine you have been selected for a present-day experiment, with a couple of twists. First, while you would not be able to negotiate whether to give up anything, you are able to negotiate what order you can give things up. Second, Job's list included three categories: possessions, family, and health. The list below is much more extensive.

Do your best to rank order the following items, with the first items on the list being those you would choose to lose first and the last items on the list those you would choose to hold on to the longest. Feel free to add to the list additional items.

Your vehicle; your house; your yard or garden; all of your other material possessions; your immediate family; your extended family; your best friend; your friendship network; your memories; your cognitive abilities; your sense of smell; sense of touch; sense of taste; sense of sight; sense of hearing; your intuition; your dominant hand; physical mobility; any other characteristics of your life that you hold dear.

Once you have rank ordered the items, do you see any pattern? Are there any commonalities of the items ranked first or last? Finally, is there a point on the list that you would decide life would not be worth living were the loss to be permanent?

SECTION II

NOTES FROM THE SACRED HEART:

Divine Warrior Training

Exercise 9: Both Masculine and Feminine

All humans have a combination of masculine and feminine qualities - no one is 100% masculine or feminine. Taoist traditions use the yin/yang symbol to illustrate the balance between the two complementary properties. The masculine property is seen as action, and the feminine property is seen as receptive (you are welcome to add other qualities as you like).

1. Surveying your life, how much of your life is more masculine and how much of your life is more feminine? Does your life feel balanced between action and being receptive? If not, how could you change your life to make it more balanced?

2. If you had no concern for what other people thought, would you add more of one of these qualities to your life? If so, is not adding that quality worth the approval you receive for being the way you are?

SECTION II

NOTES FROM THE SACRED HEART:

Exercise 10a: Holistic Model – Physical (Part 1 of 4)

These questions are intended to start you on a journey of self examination to assess where you might be out of balance from either investing too much energy into an area or not investing enough energy into an area. You are invited to expand, add to, or otherwise modify the questions to meet the needs of your journey. If you choose to work on only two areas during the time you have right now, you might want to pick the one that seems the "easiest" to examine and the one that seems the "hardest" to examine.

Physical
- Do I have a regular exercise routine?
- Using the four physical attributes of strength, stamina, speed, and balance, rank them from the least developed to the most developed.
- Do I know my body? What part(s) do I have the hardest time accepting? How can I find new ways to invite those unaccepted parts into the whole of my being?
- How do I nurture my physical body?
- How do I feed myself physically?
- What kind of do-able contract could I make with myself in regard to physical?

SECTION II

NOTES FROM THE SACRED HEART:

Exercise 10b: Holistic Model – Intellectual (Part 2 of 4)

These questions are intended to start you on a journey of self examination to assess where you might be out of balance from either investing too much energy into an area or not investing enough energy into an area. You are invited to expand, add to, or otherwise modify the questions to meet the needs of your journey. If you choose to work on only two areas during the time you have right now, you might want to pick the one that seems the "easiest" to examine and the one that seems the "hardest" to examine.

Intellectual
- In what ways do I exercise my mind?
- How do I feed myself intellectually?
- Pick one long-held belief and seek out information that contradicts it. Spend time feeling what it might be like to believe the opposite of what you believe. Then use your mind to decide whether to incorporate all, some or none of the information, developing a rational reason for rejecting it.
- Have I gotten lazy with my mind around: work, home, friends, family? Stated differently, when is the last time I was surprised (in either a positive way or negative way) by something someone did? How did I react to the event that helped my mind jump out of its ingrained neural pathways?
- What kind of do-able contract could I make with myself in regard to intellectual?

SECTION II

NOTES FROM THE SACRED HEART:

Exercise 10c: Holistic Model – Emotional (Part 3 of 4)

These questions are intended to start you on a journey of self examination to assess where you might be out of balance from either investing too much energy into an area or not investing enough energy into an area. You are invited to expand, add to, or otherwise modify the questions to meet the needs of your journey. If you choose to work on only two areas during the time you have right now, you might want to pick the one that seems the "easiest" to examine and the one that seems the "hardest" to examine.

Emotional
- In what situations do I become angry or fearful?
- For this anger or fear, is there a pattern to the timing, persons, settings, or any other factors?
- What are the beliefs or values behind that emotion or the pattern?
- Do those emotions serve me well in those settings (that is, do they help me get my needs met)?
- Would there be a stronger, more direct way to getting my needs met?
- What emotions, when expressed by others, bother me the most?
- How might I find value in a positive expression of that emotion in my life?
- What kind of do-able contract could I make with myself in regard to emotional?

SECTION II

NOTES FROM THE SACRED HEART:

Exercise 10d: Holistic Model – Spiritual (Part 4 of 4)

These questions are intended to start you on a journey of self examination to assess where you might be out of balance from either investing too much energy into an area or not investing enough energy into an area. You are invited to expand, add to, or otherwise modify the questions to meet the needs of your journey. If you choose to work on only two areas during the time you have right now, you might want to pick the one that seems the "easiest" to examine and the one that seems the "hardest" to examine.

Spiritual
- What is my relationship with the divine?
- In what ways do I foster my relationship with the divine?
- How do I communicate with the divine? Is it a two-way communication?
- Where do I find my intuition?
- How do I discern intuition from fear?
- Do I organize spiritual energy around certain named entities? God? Angels? Guides? Loved ones who have passed on?
- How might those "external" entities be reframed as part of me?

SECTION II

NOTES FROM THE SACRED HEART:

Divine Warrior Training

Exercise 11: Mirrors

Each of us acts as a mirror for the people in our lives. Like mirrors, what we reflect back to others is a reflection of ourselves. If we are distorted, clouded or dirty, the picture of others we reflect back to them has those added qualities. The best mirrors are clear and undistorted, reflecting back to you an accurate picture of how you are in the world.

Who are your best "mirrors?" Who can you count on to not only love you unconditionally, but also tell you the truth about your skills and challenges?

When you find yourself confused, disillusioned or afraid, go to one of your mirrors. Tell them the circumstances, and then ask them what you are missing. Then listen very carefully. If they are a clear, undistorted mirror, they will reflect back to you that which you have trouble seeing on your own.

SECTION II

NOTES FROM THE SACRED HEART:

Exercise 12: What Feeds You and What Drains You

Think of your life as it currently exists. We all have things that give us energy and things to which we give our energy. If we receive energy from it, it feeds us. If we give our energy to it, it drains us. Some things may do both. For those things that do both, try to determine what part of that thing feeds you and what part of it drains you.

Here are some categories (possibly overlapping) that may spur your thinking: physical, emotional, intellectual, spiritual, internal, external, man-made, natural, relationships, solitude, self-care, work, home.

What do you get lost in? (feeds you)	What do you feel obligated to do? (drains you)
1.	1.
2.	2.
3.	3.
4.	4.
5.	5.
6.	6.
7.	7.
8.	8.
9.	9.
10.	10.

SECTION II

NOTES FROM THE SACRED HEART:

Exercise 13: A Burger and a Salad

Which do you know is better for the long-term maintenance of your body, a burger or a salad? We often have an intellectual understanding of what is good for us or what is right for our bodies, but we make a different choice. When we make those choices, our emotional needs override our intellectual understanding.

What do you know is not good for you that you keep going back to? There is something in that thing or relationship that feeds you. Is the part that feeds you worth the cost of the drain on your energy?

SECTION II

NOTES FROM THE SACRED HEART:

Exercise 14: Exile

Exile is the opposite of belonging. To be exiled is to be cast out of the comfort and security of the collective. There are many forms and levels of exile, and two broad categories are internal exile and external exile.

Internal exile

In what way do you not feel a part of the collective? When have you felt different from everyone else? When have you felt misunderstood? These times can be seen as moments of internal exile, where you have set yourself apart from the collective. As you reflect on these times, notice whether these were times when you examined your values and you came to view your values as at odds with the values of the collective. Perhaps your time of internal exile was beneficial in developing your values and an individual sense of self.

External exile

Have there been times in your life where you have felt cast out of the collective? How did you respond? What was the stated reason for this exile, and how have you come to understand it? From your perspective, was it a shortcoming of your values or a shortcoming of the values of the collective?

SECTION II

NOTES FROM THE SACRED HEART:

Exercise 15: Polarities

Anything we perceive can be viewed as one end of a spectrum of possibilities. For example, a person who sees himself as shy could view the other end of the spectrum as a person who is comfortable around anyone and everyone. Pick a quality you find in yourself to examine. It might be most helpful to pick a quality you are not particularly fond of.

What is the opposite of this quality? Create a continuum, with 1 being as much of this quality as you can imagine, and 10 being as much of the opposite quality as you can imagine.

1   2   3   4   5   6   7   8   9   10

What number are you currently in the spectrum?

For a person who is a #1, list all the advantages and disadvantages of living with that much of that quality.

For a person who is a #10, list all the advantages and disadvantages of living with that much of that quality.

If, after doing the above work, you are uncomfortable with where you are on the continuum, how might you incorporate more of the opposite quality in your life? Decide on some specific steps and try them out in your life!

SECTION II

NOTES FROM THE SACRED HEART:

Divine Warrior Training

Exercise 16: On Your Heels or On Your Toes

Think about days in which you feel like an active participant in life and challenges appear as opportunities.

Now think of days in which you feel like life happens to you and challenges appear overwhelming.

Make a list of the differences between these two types of days, focusing specifically on how you cared for yourself leading up to and during the two types of days (for example, how much sleep did you get, how early did you wake, how did you feed yourself, etc.).

SECTION II

NOTES FROM THE SACRED HEART:

Exercise 17: The Problem of Evil

The following three conditions are incompatible:

God is all powerful (omnipotent)

God is all good (omnibenevolent)

Evil exists.

Many people believe each of these three concepts. If you believe them all, please use your understanding of the concepts of good and evil to explain how these three truths can co-exist in our world.

SECTION II

NOTES FROM THE SACRED HEART:

Divine Warrior Training

Exercise 18: Evil in the Spiritual World

Many people believe in benevolent or positive energies and entities in the spiritual world. People with spiritual world views report being guided or protected by "guides," "angels," or other benevolent entities. If there are benevolent spiritual entities, are there also malevolent spiritual entities? If so, how do they operate in the material world? Can a person be guided by them in the same way people are guided by benevolent spiritual entities? How does a person protect himself or herself from these malevolent spiritual entities? How does a person learn to discern between benevolent guidance and malevolent guidance?

SECTION II

NOTES FROM THE SACRED HEART:

Divine Warrior Training

Exercise 19a: Defining Evil

Many authors have provided attempts at defining or outlining the concept of evil and its sources. The quotes on this and the following page are some of the attempts. After reviewing the quotes, select three quotes which are "truest" for you and write your own definition of evil. You also might want to note the quotes which are farthest from your understanding of evil and what feels off about them.

> If only it were all so simple! If only there were evil people somewhere insidiously committing evil deeds, and it were necessary only to separate them from the rest of us and destroy them. But the line dividing good and evil cuts through the heart of every human being. And who is willing to destroy a piece of his own heart?
> - Alexander Solzhenitsyn

> The evil of our time is the loss of consciousness of evil.
> - Krishnamurti

> The spread of evil is the symptom of a vacuum. Whenever evil wins, it is only by default: by the moral failure of those who evade the fact that there can be no compromise on basic principles.
> - Ayn Rand

> I have discovered that all human evil comes from this, man's being unable to sit still in a room.
> - Blaise Pascal

> Men never do evil so completely and cheerfully as when they do it from a religious conviction.
> - Blaise Pascal

Section II

Notes from the Sacred Heart:

Divine Warrior Training

Exercise 19b: Defining Evil

Many authors have provided attempts at defining or outlining the concept of evil and its sources. The quotes on this and the following page are some of the attempts. After reviewing the quotes, select three quotes which are "truest" for you and write your own definition of evil. You also might want to note the quotes which are farthest from your understanding of evil and what feels off about them.

> All that is necessary for the triumph of evil is that good men do nothing.
> - Edmund Burke

> Evil is ... a moral entity and not a created one, an eternal and not a perishable entity: it existed before the world; it constituted the monstrous, the execrable being who was also to fashion such a hideous world. It will hence exist after the creatures which people this world.
> - Marquis de Sade

> There is nothing either good or bad, but thinking makes it so.
> - William Shakespeare

> Ignorance, the root and stem of all evil.
> - Plato

> Evil is the radiation of the human consciousness in certain transitional positions. It is not actually the sensual world that is a mere appearance; what is so is the evil of it, which, admittedly, is what constitutes the sensual world in our eyes.
> - Franz Kafka

SECTION II

NOTES FROM THE SACRED HEART:

Divine Warrior Training

Exercise 19c: Defining Evil

Many authors have provided attempts at defining or outlining the concept of evil and its sources. The quotes on this and the following page are some of the attempts. After reviewing the quotes, select three quotes which are "truest" for you and write your own definition of evil. You also might want to note the quotes which are farthest from your understanding of evil and what feels off about them.

> Evil can be got very easily and exists in quantity: the road to her is very smooth, and she lives near by. But between us and virtue the gods have placed the sweat of our brows; the road to her is long and steep, and it is rough at first; but when a man has reached the top, then she is easy to attain, although before she was hard.
> - Hesiod

> Evil is that which one believes of others. It is a sin to believe evil of others, but it is seldom a mistake.
> - H.L. (Henry Lewis) Mencken

> Evil is simply
> a grammatical error:
> a failure to leap
> the precipice
> between "he"
> and "I."
> - Linda Pastan

SECTION II

NOTES FROM THE SACRED HEART:

Exercise 19d: Defining Evil

Many authors have provided attempts at defining or outlining the concept of evil and its sources. The quotes on this and the following page are some of the attempts. After reviewing the quotes, select three quotes which are "truest" for you and write your own definition of evil. You also might want to note the quotes which are farthest from your understanding of evil and what feels off about them.

> Good and evil are essential differences of the act of the will. For good and evil pertain essentially to the will; just as truth and falsehood pertain to the reason, the act of which is distinguished essentially by the difference of truth and falsehood (according as we say that an opinion is true or false.) Consequently, good and evil volition are acts differing in species.
> - Thomas Aquinas

> Every sweet has its sour; every evil its good.
> - Ralph Waldo Emerson

> Evil when we are in its power is not felt as evil but as a necessity, or even a duty.
> - Simone Weil

> There is no explanation for evil. It must be looked upon as a necessary part of the order of the universe. To ignore it is childish, to bewail it senseless.
> - W. Somerset Maugham

SECTION II

NOTES FROM THE SACRED HEART:

Exercise 20: Absolute Evil

Whenever evil befalls us, we ought to ask ourselves, after the first suffering, how we can turn it into good. So shall we take occasion, from one bitter root, to raise perhaps many flowers.
 - Leigh Hunt

Is there a seed of good in all evil, or can evil be so negative that no good can come from it? You may want to use an event in the past to look at evil and its consequences, either a world event (the Holocaust, September 11, 2001, etc.) or a personal tragedy to examine this question. If good can come from evil, what are the conditions which make good possible?

SECTION II

NOTES FROM THE SACRED HEART:

Exercise 21: Evidence of, and Beliefs about, Evil

Each of us has developed our own understanding of and relationship to evil. Our view is developed over our entire lives. As adults, we often use our rational minds to construct our world views, developing beliefs based on our experience of the events in our lives. As children, we are often given concepts and beliefs from those we love and those concepts and beliefs are adopted in the absence of, or sometimes in spite of, evidence to the contrary.

First, list the evidence of evil based on your experience of the events in your life. Second, list the beliefs about evil you hold, both from your childhood and adulthood. Finally, examine the beliefs in light of your experiences and determine whether they are consistent or need modification or outright rejection.

SECTION II

NOTES FROM THE SACRED HEART:

Exercise 22: Making Sense of Spontaneous Remission

Spontaneous remission has been defined as the sudden disappearance of diseased tissue, and is most commonly associated with cancer. In your belief system, to what do you attribute spontaneous remission? Choose a situation you are currently struggling with. Whether you characterize the situation as physical or otherwise, what might spontaneous remission look like for that situation?

SECTION II

NOTES FROM THE SACRED HEART:

Divine Warrior Training

Exercise 23: The Empty Chair

Set a chair (or another place to sit) across from where you are sitting. Take a few minutes to meditate, closing your eyes, deepening and lengthening your breath, quieting your mind.

Now imagine you have invited someone or something that represents the divine to join you and invite them to sit in the place you have arranged for them. You may do this exercise silently to yourself or out loud. Take the time to thank them for joining you, and then take some time to listen to what they have to say to you. Engage in a conversation, as you would while talking to someone for whom you have the utmost respect. If you would like to take notes while they are talking, ask their permission.

After you have taken between 30 minutes and an hour of their valuable time, thank them again and send them on their way. If you would like, you might ask if you can set up another appointment.

SECTION II

NOTES FROM THE SACRED HEART:

Divine Warrior Training

Exercise 24: What is a Miracle?

How do you define a miracle? Do miracles happen in today's world? What are the necessary preconditions of a miracle? What would it take for a miracle to happen in your life?

SECTION II

NOTES FROM THE SACRED HEART:

Exercise 25: Breath as Healing

Breath has been called prana, a form of life force energy. There are people who believe that all healing in our body results from working with the breath. How might your relationship with your breath be limiting your healing power? How might you improve your relationship with your breath to increase your healing power?

SECTION II

NOTES FROM THE SACRED HEART:

Exercise 26: The Blessing is Next to the Wound

There is an African saying, "the blessing is next to the wound." If you were to look for a "blessing" next to your "wound" (or chronic condition, or trauma, or whatever situation you are struggling with), what would you find?

SECTION II

NOTES FROM THE SACRED HEART:

Divine Warrior Training

Exercise 27: Illness as a Metaphor

Choose a chronic condition or aspect of your health that you would like to change. Imagine that this situation you have chosen is a messenger sent from your body to your consciousness. What might it be trying to say to you? How can the situation be seen as a representation of what might be off in your life, in one or all of the following areas: spiritual, emotional, physical, intellectual?

Take some time to simply listen to the situation and what it wants to say to you rather than trying to fix or mask the symptoms. What might you do differently in your life to respond to the message from your body?

SECTION II

NOTES FROM THE SACRED HEART:

Divine Warrior Training

Exercise 28: Laughter is the Best Medicine

Norman Cousins is said to have healed himself of a chronic heart condition through the use of laughter, incorporating as much loving laughter into his life as he could.

How much do you laugh? Are there ways you can reconstruct your life to include more laughter? Are there ways you view your life that keep you from laughter? Were there times in your life that had more laughter? If so, what has changed and how can you move back into that type of life space?

List as many easy, low cost or no cost ways you can think of to increase the laughter in your life, and then choose to implement them.

SECTION II

NOTES FROM THE SACRED HEART:

Divine Warrior Training

Exercise 29: Speaking Authentically #1

Think of the people in your life. Make a list of the people in your life to whom you would like to say something but have chosen not to speak. What keeps you from speaking your mind to them in love? What do you fear losing? Why are you holding back?

SECTION II

NOTES FROM THE SACRED HEART:

DIVINE WARRIOR TRAINING

EXERCISE 30: SPEAKING AUTHENTICALLY #2

Do you say things about people that you would not say to their face? If so, how does this behavior fit with your understanding of authenticity? How does this behavior benefit the person about whom you are speaking? What value can you set for yourself to live into that brings more love and authenticity into the world?

SECTION II

NOTES FROM THE SACRED HEART:

Divine Warrior Training

Exercise 31: Your Persona versus Your True Self

Take a sheet of paper and pretend it is a mask. Hold it up to your face and on the side facing you, the inside, list the values and "true self" living inside of you. On the side facing away from you, the outside, list the "you" everyone sees, the values and "persona" you present to the world.

The degree to which the lists are the same or different is the level of your authenticity. Are there changes you would like to make? Are there successes you would like to celebrate?

SECTION II

NOTES FROM THE SACRED HEART:

Divine Warrior Training

Exercise 32: Speaking Truth

The Quakers have a saying, "Speak truth to power." To this phrase, I believe it is important to add "with love." As "speak truth to power with love," the phrase becomes a triangle of ideals to which we can apsire in our dealings with others:

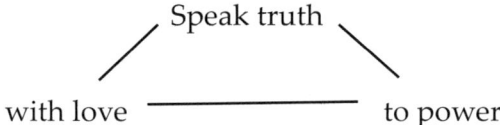

with love — to power

1. Which of these three ideals is the easiest for you right now?

2. Which of these three ideals is the hardest for you right now?

3. Why is it important to have all three existing together? From your experience, what happens when you have only one or two out of the three?

SECTION II

NOTES FROM THE SACRED HEART:

Divine Warrior Training

Exercise 33: Giving It All Up

What area of your life have you found easy to surrender or give up control to the divine? Name an area of your life you have found difficult to surrender or give up control to the divine. What is the difference between these two areas?

SECTION II

NOTES FROM THE SACRED HEART:

Exercise 34: The Divine Moves in Mysterious Ways

If you believe the divine is active in your life, is it easier for you to celebrate the "good" things that happen than it is to endure the "bad" things that happen? Could events you place in the "good" category and events you place in the "bad" category both be gifts from the divine? Why or why not?

SECTION II

NOTES FROM THE SACRED HEART:

Divine Warrior Training

Exercise 35: Be Still

Be still and know that I AM.
- Psalms 46:10

This scripture has three ideals to focus upon:

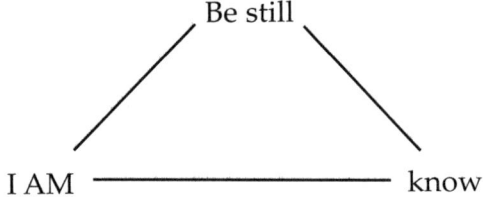

1. Which of these three ideals do you have the most difficulty living into?

2. Which of these three ideals is the easiest for you?

3. Are they all three essential, or can you come to a balance point in your life without one of the three? If you believe so, describe how.

SECTION II

NOTES FROM THE SACRED HEART:

DIVINE WARRIOR TRAINING

Exercise 36: Who Cares?!

What would you do with your life if it didn't matter to you where you slept, what you wore, what kind of car you drove, where your next meal came from and what other people thought of you? What if the divine is asking you to do that right now? Would you do it? Why or why not?

SECTION II

NOTES FROM THE SACRED HEART:

Exercise 37: Assessing Your Connection to the Divine

Review the following statements and indicate which one(s) you have the most difficulty believing or living:

1. The divine is all loving.
2. The divine loves me in particular.
3. The divine is sending me guidance all the time.
4. The divine's guidance for me is everywhere and in everything.
5. I do a good job of hearing the guidance from the divine.
6. I do a good job of deciding what the divine's guidance means to me.
7. I do a good job of acting on the divine's guidance.

After you have selected the statement(s) which is(are) hardest for you, spend some time in self-reflection looking at what is blocking you from living into that(those) statement(s).

SECTION II

NOTES FROM THE SACRED HEART:

Exercise 38: Finding the Weak Link

Discerning divine will can be seen as a series of steps:

1. the process of listening
2. receiving the content of what is being conveyed
3. attaching the correct meaning of the content for your life
4. acting on the guidance received

Which of these is hardest for you? Which is easiest? Are there more steps you would add? How might you improve on your discernment using these categories?

SECTION II

NOTES FROM THE SACRED HEART:

Divine Warrior Training

Exercise 39: Rules for Discernment

Some people use "the rule of 3's" for discernment: if a message or topic comes to them three times, then it is something they need to pay attention to. Does the rule of 3's work for you? Do you have other rules that you have discovered to discern divine will? What are those rules? How reliable are they?

Notes from the Sacred Heart:

SECTION II

Exercise 40: Choosing a Path of Love

Choose a part of your life in which you would like some divine guidance. What choices of actions do you see as possibilities for this situation? Use brainstorming to list as many as you can.

Now set the list you have generated aside. If you were to choose a path of love, what kind of questions would you want to ask about the items on the list to determine which is the path of love?

Here are some possible questions to get you started:

- Which choice holds the possibility of the least amount of harm to others?
- Which choice holds the possibility of the least amount of harm to myself?
- Which choice expands me?
- Which choice may help heal a past wound?

Come up with your own questions, then go back to your list and see if the questions help you get clear about which path to choose.

SECTION II

NOTES FROM THE SACRED HEART:

Divine Warrior Training

Exercise 41: The Divine 2 x 4

Can you recall a message from the divine that you finally heard "loud and clear?" Reflect back on your life to the time *before* you got the message loud and clear and see if there were other, more subtle messages or signs that you did not attend to. If so, how might you change the way you listen to the divine to be able to hear the next message before it gets so loud?

SECTION II

NOTES FROM THE SACRED HEART:

Divine Warrior Training

Exercise 42: Tuning in to the Messages all around You

Take a moment to get centered. Allow your perceptual focus to become unfocused, not using any of your senses to focus on anything in particular. After spending a few moments unfocused, allow your senses to be drawn to some thing that draws your attention. Attend to that thing and the sensations it brings fully and with no distractions. Attend to that thing as long as it takes to allow it to bring you three messages for your life in this moment.

Section II

Notes from the Sacred Heart:

SECTION II

AFTERWORD

HERE WE ARE AT THE END OF THE BOOK, and at the beginning of a new journey - a new chapter of our lives. As stated at the beginning of this book, the path of a divine warrior has challenges and rewards. The beauty of life is that we are often provided an opportunity to try again after falling short and we always carry with us that drive to the divine, that inner spark, that helps us reengage our choices. And remember we are not alone in walking the path. Reach up and reach out. Step up and step out. Manifest the divine in this world. I am at your service. With divine love, Tom

Quick Order Form

To order additional copies of **Divine Warrior Training**, visit our website: www.innersparkpress.com

You may also order additional copies by mail. Please send your order to:

    Innerspark Press
    P.O. Box 2244
    Bloomington, IN 47402-2244
    USA

Please send the following quantity of books and/or CDs:
_____
_____
_____

I understand that I may return any of them for a full refund - for any reason, no questions asked.

Sales Tax: Please add 7% for products shipped to Indiana addresses.

Shipping and handling: Domestic addresses, please add $4.00 for first item and $2.00 for each additional product. International orders, please add $9.00 for first item, $5.00 for each additional item.

Please send FREE information on:
__ Speaking/Seminars   __ Spirituality Services
__ Consulting on writing and publishing

Name: _____

Address: _____

City, State and Zip: _____

Telephone: _____ Email: _____

Quick Order Form

To order additional copies of **Divine Warrior Training**, visit our website: **www.innersparkpress.com**

You may also order additional copies by mail. Please send your order to:

        Innerspark Press
        P.O. Box 2244
        Bloomington, IN 47402-2244
        USA

Please send the following quantity of books and/or CDs:
_____
_____
_____

I understand that I may return any of them for a full refund - for any reason, no questions asked.

Sales Tax: Please add 7% for products shipped to Indiana addresses.

Shipping and handling: Domestic addresses, please add $4.00 for first item and $2.00 for each additional product. International orders, please add $9.00 for first item, $5.00 for each additional item.

Please send FREE information on:
__ Speaking/Seminars   __ Spirituality Services
__ Consulting on writing and publishing

Name: _____

Address: _____

City, State and Zip: _____

Telephone: _____ Email: _____

photo © 2007 by Kathryn Robinson

At 21-years-old, Thomas F. Capshew had a crisis of faith. He was within one year of graduating to become a minister, double majoring in Bible and Biblical Languages. Unable to reconcile the teachings of the church in which he was raised with a loving God, he transferred to another school and left the church. Since then, he has studied many faith traditions including Hindu and Buddhist philosophies, as well as indigenous traditions. This book brings him full circle, a circle embracing the common essence of all faith traditions.

Dr. Capshew earned an undergraduate degree in Psychology and a law degree from Indiana University. He earned a Masters in Social Work and a doctorate from Florida State University. Dr. Capshew has enjoyed successful careers as an attorney and a social work professor. He currently practices, trains, and writes in the area of spirituality and the healing arts. He brings to his life the mind of an attorney, the heart of a social worker, and the soul of a mystic.